C. V. WHITNEY **High Peaks**

The University Press of Kentucky | Lexington

ISBN: 0–8131–1357–1

Library of Congress Catalog Card Number: 76–51158

Copyright © 1977 by The University Press of Kentucky

A statewide cooperative scholarly publishing agency
serving Berea College, Centre College of Kentucky,
Eastern Kentucky University, The Filson Club,
Georgetown College, Kentucky Historical Society,
Kentucky State University, Morehead State University,
Murray State University, Northern Kentucky University,
Transylvania University, University of Kentucky,
University of Louisville, and Western Kentucky University.

Editorial and Sales Offices: Lexington, Kentucky 40506

Contents

Foreword

ON MEETING Cornelius Vanderbilt Whitney, one is impressed by the incredible youthfulness, the vitality of the man, and the vividness of his conversation. A vital, vivid spirit also characterizes much of "Sonny" Whitney's writing. He recently worked two years on an autobiography of a more or less traditional sort. Ultimately "I abandoned it because I don't live in the past," he says, "and so I could not recall sufficient details for a conventional biography."

Fortunately, he hit upon a new and far more satisfactory plan, concentrating on the "high peaks" of a varied career. This more selective method gave the author an opportunity to stress the colorful, avoid the dull, and develop a pattern similar to the short-story techniques he has admired since boyhood. It likewise enabled him to fuse present and past in many particulars.

Mr. Whitney's achievements in the raising and racing of Thoroughbred horses, in establishing Florida's Marineland, and in directing C. V. Whitney Industries reflect only three of his numerous interests. They are part of the 1977 Whitney personality, just as are the Buffalo Bill Historical Center in Wyoming and the Performing Arts Center at Saratoga Springs.

"Generally speaking," Mr. Whitney points out, "movies and TV present rich persons—millionaires— very differently from the life I've led." In *High Peaks,* he relates some things one millionaire has done—real episodes and achievements, not caricatures or figments of fancy. And he presents a kaleidoscope of American life during the first three-quarters of the twentieth century.

In several important areas, he shares the pleasures and concerns of legions of fellow-citizens. He loves the outdoors, for example, deals happily and constructively with problems of advancing years, and finds relaxation in such things as "exploring the countryside, wherever I am, and taking my wife and children along for a picnic or lunch at an inn."

Through his father, Mr. Whitney's Kentucky connections go far back. But it has been in the last eighteen years that he and Mrs. Whitney and their children have actually lived on their horse farm near Lexington. He has taken, and continues to take, a deep interest in Kentucky life and land. Natural Bridge, Cumberland Falls, Jenny Wiley, and other Kentucky state parks are —not occasionally but steadily—objects of his visits and admiration.

Philanthropy, the constructive drive, versatility, exuberance, courage, and taste are among the characteristics appearing between the lines of this volume. And throughout is seen the sparkle of an affirmative American.

HOLMAN HAMILTON
Emeritus Professor of History
University of Kentucky

Preface

I LIVE in the present and look to the future. So I have selected only those memories which remain as vivid and exciting as when they occurred, recently or many years ago. Hence the title: *High Peaks*.

Well then, who am I? I am that lucky guy born with the proverbial silver spoon in his mouth, who nevertheless made careers in big business, civic and military service, and competitive sports with the outdoors as the vital component of all of these. My favorite quotation is from David in Psalm 121, "I will lift mine eyes unto the hills whence cometh my help." I have needed God's help many times in my arduous life, and I am never afraid to pray for guidance, to thank Him for favors received, and to ask forgiveness when I stray—for to err is only human, to forgive, divine.

My American ancestor, Jon Whitney, came to Massachusetts in 1635. There he held important town offices in Worcester, apparently lived honorably, and had a wife and seven sons. I am a descendant of Richard, to whom the old gentleman left in his will "ten acres of land, two cows and a great sea chest." I confess that this modest legacy has grown considerably.

I have seen the end of the Victorian era, the roaring twenties, the pioneering thirties, the fateful forties, the happy fifties and sixties, and the turbulent seventies. I have known and worked with many of the important figures of those times, from presidents, kings and generals, to movie stars, directors, fighters, sports champions, pioneers, politicians, and beautiful people. I am doing the same today.

So now on with the *High Peaks*, for time and tide wait for no man.

High Peaks

1 | From Ice Cream on Sundays to the Wild Blue Yonder

MY BOYHOOD HOME was a glorious country estate of some thousand acres near Old Westbury, Long Island. It was a big red brick house situated on top of a hill, with rolling green pastures to the south and a wild forest to the north. Dominating the estate was a brick tower that stood two hundred feet high with a windmill on top, supplying us with water from a well in the sands below. We had a stable full of horses, a good-sized kennel, an outdoor tennis court and swimming pool, and an indoor gymnasium replete with bowling alley and squash court. And those rolling green pastures to the south of the house were dotted with fruit trees, a huge vegetable garden, a herd of Jersey cows, and lots of chickens, pigs, and pigeons. In those days there was always ample help to maintain an estate of that size.

It was all very grand, I must say, except for my spartan quarters in the attic. I, the middle child and only son, had a tiny bedroom with a cot, a small bathroom adjoining, and an empty storeroom beyond. No one else lived in the attic, for which I was very grateful, for I prized my privacy. My sisters, Flora and Barbara, and their French governess occupied sumptuous bedrooms with a large playroom on the second floor. My sisters reveled in their surroundings every bit as much as I did in mine. In those days boys were never roomed within striking distance of girls.

My boyhood chums lived on adjacent estates and enjoyed the same general life-style.

Summers were spent in Newport, and we also enjoyed the 85,000-acre Whitney Park in the Adirondacks, a very primitive and wild area where I was taught to canoe, fish, camp out in log lean-tos, and sleep on balsam boughs under starry skies.

Our house in town was a brownstone mansion at Sixty-eighth Street and Fifth Avenue, with a great marble staircase and a ballroom. It had been built by my grandfather, Secretary of the Navy William C. Whitney. I roller-skated to and from Miss Bove's School on East Forty-ninth Street between Fifth and Madison Avenues, a round trip of some two miles. After school my friends and I would take off for Central Park, which in those days often appeared to be the exclusive terrain of school children. We would gang up and rove far and wide, exploring. So you might say we led a rustic life in the metropolis with roller skates added to speed things up a bit.

The zoo was a favorite hangout in the park, and there we would spend our weekly allowance of twenty-five cents on peanuts and popcorn. Rarely did we spend our money riding the Fifth Avenue bus, although that's what we were given the money for each week. Still, I did hop the bus one day (can't remember why since it wasn't raining or snowing) and when it stopped at Sixty-eighth Street, the driver, a garrulous fellow, suddenly blurted out, "The mansion you see in front of you belongs to the Whitney family. They're millionaires.

They have ice cream for lunch every Sunday." I hopped off the bus and stood on the curb, not moving, until it pulled away. I didn't want anyone to associate *me* with the brownstone mansion. It wasn't that I was ashamed. I just didn't like being singled out and made to feel all that different. And furthermore, the driver's information was inaccurate. We usually had tapioca or rice pudding on Sunday. It was only on birthdays, Christmas, and Easter that we got ice cream. I never rode the Fifth Avenue bus again. From that day on, every cent of my twenty-five cents was spent on peanuts and popcorn in Central Park.

Anyway, buses and automobiles didn't interest me. They were much too confining. My passion was for the outdoors and the creatures who lived there. I zealously studied books on animals, birds, and reptiles. When I was a boy, Central Park abounded with squirrels, pigeons, chucks, and wild birds. In a vacant room in our home in Old Westbury, I kept a collection of birds' eggs, each identified and catalogued. The family knew about my egg collection, but nothing about my collection of snakes. That is why I prized my privacy up there in the attic. My very special pet was a three-foot king snake for whom I trapped mice which I fed him regularly. One Sunday when I must have been full of mischief, I coiled him around my neck and marched downstairs where luncheon was about to be served. The huge dining room was filled with friends of my parents and to this day I can recall their open-mouthed shock at the sight of my snake and me. My father promptly ordered me to my room where I spent the rest of the afternoon. I sat on my cot staring down at the bread and water sent up for my lunch, mindful of the fact that downstairs my sisters were probably eating ice cream after a delicious turkey with cranberry sauce.

At age twelve, I was sent to Groton School in Massachusetts, the faraway state in which old Jon Whitney had settled back there in the early seventeenth century. My father had attended Groton before me and so it was taken for granted that I would follow in his footsteps. That was all right with me, especially since my cousin Douglas Burden was also going there. Our gang was beginning to scatter, however, with my close pal Tommy Hitchcock taking off for St. Paul's in New Hampshire, and lots of my Newport friends registering at St. George's in Rhode Island.

I was not a dedicated student but I devoted my energies to sports: football, crew, and baseball. Fortunately for me, our headmaster, the Reverend Endicott Peabody, loved athletics and so I squeezed by. Still, in fairness to myself, I should add here that I was also on the debating team, took piano lessons, played the drums in the school band, and rang the bells in the chapel tower. By the time I was graduated in June, 1917, I had even spent many hours in the school library. To anyone seeing me there, I might have appeared to be something of a scholar. The books that riveted my attention, however, were not the classics but out-and-out adventure stories having to do with exploration in primitive areas. I vowed that some day, somehow, I would explore those faraway places.

I was enrolled in the freshman class at Yale in the autumn and then returned home to Old Westbury where I was greeted with warmth and affection. After all, in graduating from Groton I had done what was expected of me. No one, including me, suspected that very shortly I would do something that was totally unexpected.

A war was being fought overseas and things were not going any too happily for our friends, the English and the French. All around me the people I cherished most were doing something in the war effort. My mother, who loved France dearly, had organized a volunteer nursing group. And I soon discovered that my pal Tommy Hitchcock had joined a voluntary air force unit called the Lafayette Escadrille. I had an overpowering urge to get involved, although I was too young to join the army. The best I could do under the circumstances then was to enlist in a summer training camp for lads under nineteen that was located on Plum Island at the eastern tip of Long Island Sound. Although any sort of military training was novel to me, the summers I had spent at our camp in the Adirondacks helped. Rugged marches, living in a tent, and shooting a rifle posed no problems for me, and by the time the camp was disbanded late in summer, I had attained the rank of corporal. After that, with our family doctor's help, I served in St. Luke's hospital in New York City as an apprentice to a surgeon. I detested this work but plugged away at it nonetheless, figuring it might lead to a job with the ambulance corps in France. By this time my mother was with an ambulance unit in France, and Tommy Hitchcock was over there too. So I couldn't wait to get there myself. I began reading in the press about the newly organized Army Signal Corps, the air force branch of the regular army, and I made up my mind to enlist. I wanted to be a fighter pilot. One day, without a word to my family, I packed a bag and took a train to Washington, D.C., where the U.S. Army Signal Corps had its enlistment offices.

I didn't have the price of a hotel room, so I had arranged—without my father's knowledge—to stay with my uncle, Congressman James Wadsworth. I telephoned him just before leaving Old Westbury and his voice radiated hospitality. "Stay as long as you wish," he said. I arrived at his fine house late in the afternoon, had supper, and retired early since I wanted to get to the enlistment office before it opened at 8:00 A.M.

The physical examination came first and, being young and strong, I was doing well until the examining physician discovered that my adenoids left something to be desired. "Take them out," I said, without a moment's hesitation. I think now that that probably sounded more like an order than a request. Perhaps I was already beginning to feel military. At any rate, the good doctor obliged. He laid me on a table and, without giving me an anesthetic, he proceeded to take them out! After a very brief rest, I was to continue with the next steps in the examination for enlistment, the eye and color tests. Feeling slightly dizzy but no less determined, I came face to face with that wretched chart with all the different colored ribbons attached to it. I wasn't exactly color blind, but I did have my troubles with color identification. So I wasn't too surprised when I failed the color test.

In the front office, an officer both cheered and depressed me. Convinced that shock from my impromptu adenoidal operation had caused me to flunk the color test, he guaranteed me that it would be arranged for me to take the test again—and since I was under eighteen years of age I must secure my father's written consent to enlist. "Good day and good luck," he said, and I went back to the Wadsworth home where I promptly called Western Union and sent my father a telegram asking him to please wire his consent to the enlistment office.

Meanwhile, after dinner I huddled with my cousin Evie, telling her about my troubles with color identification. Evie, who was about my age, took charge at once. She told me she had a girl friend who, like me, was color weak and her friend had a color chart. Evie would go and borrow it at once, which she did, and when she came back I was delighted to see that it was the identical chart I had grappled with so unsuccessfully earlier in the day. Sitting beside me Evie said, "I'll tell you the colors and you memorize them." She did . . . I did . . . after which we both concluded that next time I was certain to pass the color test with flying colors, so to speak. All I needed now was my father's consent.

That night I had a hard time falling asleep. If father didn't consent, what would I do? Up till now, I'd never been denied anything important to me. And this was important, terribly important. I knew one thing: if my father didn't give me his consent, I wouldn't return home and I would no longer love and respect him. Having come to that decision, I finally dozed off.

The next morning Evie was waiting for me, the color chart in her lap, and we resumed our practice. We were still at it when the phone rang at noon. It was the enlistment officer and he had good news. My father had wired his consent. Would I come down to the office at three o'clock? I assured him I would be there punctually. And when I left for my three o'clock appointment, Evie saw me to the door and patting my shoulder, told me she just knew I was going to pass the test. "Tonight we'll all celebrate," she added.

And pass I did, the color chart no longer a problem. After which I filled out all the necessary papers and was told to report for ground school training at Princeton University on October first.

That evening the Wadsworths gave me a marvelous dinner and toasted me with champagne. I shall always associate the pop of that champagne cork with what had to be my first important and independent decision, one that literally changed my life.

Until then, you see, I had lived in a very comfortable world but an extremely small one, shared with friends who, like me, represented the so-called upper stratum of society. Physically I was tough but I actually knew little about life outside my own limited area. Well, now I was about to find out all about it as I progressed from Princeton University to army air force training fields in Texas—Love Field in Dallas and the Benbrook and Hicks Fields in Fort Worth. After nine months, I had mastered every trick and stunt and maneuver the airplanes of that era were capable of. I was commissioned a second lieutenant, then first lieutenant and chief instructor in advanced fighter tactics. When the war ended, I was on overseas orders and Captain Eddie Rickenbacker chose me one of the five top fighter pilots in the United States. In one year, I felt I had become an adult. I had made friends from all parts of the country and all walks of life and I could hold my own with them. Now I felt ready to really step out on my own. And the time was ripe. It was a great time to be young.

2 | Living It Up

I WAS midway through my career at Yale when the twenties exploded on the scene. I think it's fair to say I was more than ready for them. The pace was fast and exciting and I was young, healthy, and not *too* bogged down with serious thoughts.

My career at Yale pretty much followed the pattern of my career at Groton. Athletics first (this time rowing—and I made the varsity crew), studies second. I majored in anthropology, but the courses I enjoyed most were American and English literature. As a result of getting five of my compositions published in the Yale literary magazine, I was elected a member of the Elizabethan Club. So much for my scholarship.

Socially, I was very active. I didn't go steady until my senior year, however; in the meantime, I played the field—society girls, stage celebrities, and, well, all sorts.

Came graduation and, to my great surprise, on my very first evening home my father said, "Son, why don't you go to Europe for the summer? I'm sure your uncle would welcome you in Hungary. And you should visit France and Italy and have a good educational vacation because after that, I'm putting you to work for the Metals Exploration Company in Comstock, Nevada."

"Papa," I said, "it sounds great, but I don't have any money."

My father patted my shoulder and allowed that he would give me $2,000 for the trip.

So I started to plan. I checked to see what Tommy Hitchcock was doing for the summer and found that he was going to Dinard in northern France to stay with Fred Prince and play polo. Tommy said he knew that Prince, an old friend of mine as well, would welcome me. Why didn't I join them?

Next I got in touch with my mother's sister, Gladys Sczechenyi, and she invited me to visit her and her husband, my Uncle Lazlo, in Budapest in September. She said we would all go for a stag hunt in the Carpathian Mountains. "Bring hunting clothes. And," she added, "a tuxedo. Budapest has lots of parties in September." I said I would bring hunting clothes and my tuxedo and furthermore, I would arrive on September first so as not to miss anything.

I also discovered that two of my best college friends would be in Paris in August, and it was agreed that we would try and hook up there and see the town.

I finally managed to get two suitcases packed and find my way via ocean liner and train to Fred Prince's house where I was royally welcomed, although it proved hardly the educational type of visit my father had in mind. In the mornings we exercised ponies and in the afternoon played polo. The evenings were spent gambling in the casino, something I had never done before. Fortunately, I spoke French fluently, for my sisters had been reared by a French governess. The big games at the casino were baccarat and chemin de fer. I learned both the hard way—by losing.

Then one evening I got into serious trouble. I was

in the hole to the tune of $1,500, which meant I would have to return home at once and abandon the rest of the vacation—something that most certainly wouldn't sit too well with Father. Standing with my hands plunged like weights in my pockets, I heard a voice behind me. "Hey, Sonny, fancy seeing you here! Are you winning a lot of money?" I turned round and faced Bob Wren, a tennis-playing friend of my father's.

"You bet I am," I lied.

"Okay, son," he said, taking out his wallet. "Here's a thousand bucks. You play with it and we'll go fifty-fifty on the profits."

Play with it I did and my luck miraculously turned round and I quit after winning $5,000 clear. My share now safely in my pocket, I was $1,000 richer than when I started to play that evening. Mr. Wren treated me to champagne at the bar, and I had sense enough to go straight to bed.

Shortly after my good fortune at the casino, I made my farewells to Fred Prince and Tommy Hitchcock and boarded the train for Paris. I had reserved a room at a small hotel on the Rue de Rivoli. My two pals from Yale were already there and so for the next two weeks we three lived it up.

During the day we visited all the historic places in and around that fabulous city. I spent hours in the Louvre and art shops. In one art shop, I bought my first oil paintings. The great court painter Oudrey had painted the two favorite hunting dogs of King Louis XV, and those paintings are still among my most prized possessions.

At night we explored the Montmartre district: all

the cabarets, dance halls, bistros, and honky tonks, mixing with the performers and bar girls. As September approached, I must admit I hated the thought of leaving Paris. I was sure that Budapest would be an anticlimax. How wrong I turned out to be!

My uncle, Count Lazlo Sczechenyi, was in the top rung of Hungarian society at that time. The Communists had been soundly defeated after World War I and Hungary was still a monarchy ruled by an emperor. But few Americans (myself included) knew very much about the Central European countries. And as I rocked along on the legendary Orient Express from Paris to Budapest, I marveled at the incredibly beautiful countryside and with the fickleness of youth began to forget Paris as I concentrated on this next port of call.

I was met at the station by a liveried chauffeur and driven in a yellow Rolls Royce to the beautiful town house of my uncle where he, Aunt Gladys, and their three daughters warmly welcomed me. A couple of days later, we traveled by stagecoach to their hunting lodge at Ramata situated in a remote valley, stopping each night en route at one of their friends' country estates where we ate heartily and were entertained by gypsy singers.

During our stay in Ramata, Uncle Lazlo took me with him each morning in search of the famous stags, somewhat similar to our western elk, that roam those wooded and rocky mountains. One day we came to a clearing in a valley and found ourselves facing a small hewn-log house with smoke cheerily curling up from its stone chimney. Uncle Lazlo said to me, "Sonny, I want to see if you could get along if you were alone and lost. I'll hide behind a tree while you go and knock on the door of that house. Tell whoever answers that you're lost and ask them how you can get back to Ramata. Do you understand?"

I strode off with my rifle slung across my shoulder. I knocked loudly on the door and presently a middle-aged woman in peasant clothes half opened it and peered out at me. Then she opened it wider, stepped outside and said something to me in Hungarian. I bowed deeply as I launched into a voluble harangue in bad German, good French, and a lot of arm waving. When I paused for breath, the woman burst into laughter and said, in good English, "Master Sonny, you don't recognize me? I was your nurse two summers in Newport." She walked towards me and took me by the hand. "Come in and warm yourself by the fire."

I heard a roar of laughter from Uncle Lazlo who came running out from behind a tree to join us. I admit I had not recognized her but soon we were fast friends over a tray of delicious cakes and cups of coffee served in front of a cheerful fire. This charming encounter was the highlight of the stag hunt as far as I was concerned for I never got so much as a shot at that elusive animal.

What a gala party the Sczechenyis gave the night we arrived back in Budapest! The elite of Hungary arrived at the house—diamonds blazing, medals gleaming—for supper, dancing, and musical entertainment by the most famous gypsy group in the country. I had a marvelous time and stayed up most of the night.

At luncheon the next day, Uncle Lazlo announced to me, *sotto voce*, that he had another festive evening set aside for me. But this time it would be just the two of us and friends of his. "Be ready at eight and wear your tux," he said. "My valet will have it laid out for you."

As usual, I was ready on the dot. We were driven in the yellow Rolls Royce to a friend's castle. There a large ballroom was filled with men and girls in flowery evening dresses. I thought the scene—the great room, the lights of rococo chandeliers reflected in the polished floor, the distinguished-looking men, and the attractive girls—looked very inviting. Uncle Lazlo whispered to me, "You will recognize most of the men, but tonight we are out with our girl friends. Our wives know it, and I suspect they're glad to be rid of us for an evening." He indicated a pretty young blonde across the room. "Your date is an actress who is unattached at the moment. I see her over there. Come along and I'll introduce you." As we started across the great room, he whispered, "She's from Vienna."

And what a charmer she was: blue eyes and young and vivacious. The gypsy group of the previous night was in full swing, and in minutes we were dancing in the ballroom. She spoke French perfectly and English well enough, and needless to say I was again most grateful for my sisters' French governess.

If anything, this party was more gracious and glamorous than the one of the evening before. The men I met greeted me warmly with invitations: to go shooting, boating on the Danube, and so on. But I had to decline for I had reservations to leave for Venice by train the next night. Which meant that I also had to say no to my date's invitation to join her the following evening and be her escort after the theatre to a small party in the country.

"Where are you going, my American boyfriend?" she asked, managing to look genuinely disappointed.

"To Venice and then to Rome," I replied, more than a little sad.

"Are you going alone?" she whispered.

"Oh yes," I said. "I'm meeting some friends in Venice."

"I wish I could go with you," she sighed, "but I can't. I must return to Vienna for my theatre engagement. Too bad, for I like you."

"I'm sorry too," I said, "but perhaps we will meet again." And so we parted, and so ended the high peak of my first European trip. I enjoyed Paris and Venice and Rome, but Budapest had been something special. I had seen Hungary in her proud heyday before the evils of Communism divided her. I had been a guest at the homes of some of her oldest families, and I had been treated with warmth and good will. Small wonder that my first European trip, and especially Hungary, remains a vivid memory.

3 | Viva Mexico!

I CAN truthfully say that I made myself a millionaire by pyramiding an investment of $3,150. This of course was the American dream. And it started with my going out west, just as Horace Greeley had urged all young men to do.

After my European holiday, my father—true to his promise—shipped me west to work for the Metals Exploration Company in Comstock, Nevada. The company, which he owned, was reworking one of the great silver mines of that area that had been abandoned in the 1890s for lack of ore. But it seemed a prospector had recently discovered a rich new vein and now the company had acquired the mining rights, built a modern mill, and operations were again under way.

Mr. Rock Channing, president of the company, met me at Comstock and told me I was beginning work underground as a mucker, the most menial job to be had. A mucker wears overalls and a steel helmet with a flashlight attached since he works often in the most remote and darkest tunnels, some so small, in fact, that he sometimes has to work in a half-crouch. His tools are a pickax, shovel, and often a wheelbarrow. Some of the work stopes in the Comstock were so hot that every hour a mucker was laid out on a slab of ice to enable him to recover enough to finish out his eight-hour shift. Add to all that the fact that dynamite blasts underground sometimes knock a man to his knees, and you can see why it was lucky for me that I was young and physically tough.

Well, I survived as a mucker and went on to finish out my year as a sampler, then on a night shift in the mill, and finally in the foreman's office computing the ore reserves on hand. I had no special privileges and received the same salary as the other men in similar positions. Came the end of the year and I was promoted to the company's main office in San Francisco to head a department of exploration to acquire other properties, for the Comstock was running out of ore.

On one of my trips in search of mines, Mr. Channing and I went to Sonora, Mexico, to inspect an enormous irrigation project in the Yaqui Valley. The Richardson Construction Company, in which my father had a one-third interest, owned one million acres of delta land through which the Yaqui River flowed west from the high mountains into the Gulf of California. A dam had been built to divert the water to irrigate this desert land, which was as fertile as the Nile delta in Egypt when water was put on it.

The only sign of civilization in this whole vast area was the tiny village of Cajeme composed of adobe houses and dirt streets. The hills surrounding Cajeme were inhabited by the still savage and warlike tribes of Yaqui Indians, making it a forbidden land to the Mexican and German settlers in the valley.

Mr. Channing and I stayed there for a week, exploring the potential of this project. We met General Alvaro Obregon, governor of Sonora, who later became president of Mexico. The general owned several thousand acres in the valley and of course was greatly interested in the future of the area. Puffing a fine cigar, he told us that, in his opinion, if it were fully developed —and by that he meant if a large dam were built to store enough water to irrigate the entire valley—the Yaqui Valley could become as important to Mexico as the Nile Valley is to Egypt. The general was a friendly, outgoing man full of enthusiasm. He had big ideas and fortunately, he—and they—made a lasting impression on me.

A year later I was back in New York City in a small office on Wall Street. I was installed there by my father who had decided it was high time that his son and heir learned the ways of banking and high finance. I was twenty-six, had served in the army, worked hard in a mine, and now I was ready to try a totally new way of life. The stock market crash was a few years into the future so Wall Street and New Yorkers were still full of optimism for the future.

One bright day my father's secretary, a Mr. Regan, telephoned me to ask that I be at my father's office at three o'clock. This happened very seldom and usually meant that I had done something wrong. This time it proved otherwise. As I sat on the other side of his very imposing desk, my father told me that he was resigning from the boards of the Guaranty Trust Company, the Metropolitan Opera Company, the Museum of Natural History, and the Metals Exploration Company, and that he wished me to serve in his place. Of the four, it was the last that struck the most responsive chord in me, bringing back memories of the time I had spent in the mine in Nevada and later exploring Mexico. At any rate, I felt proud that father wished me to serve in his place and I heartily agreed to do so. He was very businesslike about the entire matter and suggested that on my way out I drop by his secretary's office to discuss details of exactly how I should proceed.

As I entered Mr. Regan's office, he was in conversation on the telephone and I overheard the following: "Mr. Whitney has decided to sell his one-third interest in the Richardson Construction Company. You know, that outfit which owns a million acres of land in a place called the Yaqui Valley somewhere in Sonora, Mexico. He's put a half-million dollars into it and hasn't received anything from it and he's fed up. The certificates of ownership are in my office and I want you to take them across the river tomorrow and sell them on the over-the-counter market."

Mr. Regan hung up and greeted me cordially. I only half heard what he had to tell me, for my memory was busy replaying a scene with General Obregon. Mr. Regan was talking, but it was the general I was hearing as he enthusiastically described the great possibilities of the Yaqui Valley if it were properly developed. While Mr. Regan droned on, assuming I was paying full attention, I was thinking to myself: "I have about seven thousand dollars in my bank account. Will that be enough to buy the certificates of ownership my father wants to sell?" I had no idea, but I was certainly intending to find out.

I rushed back downtown on the subway to my office where my secretary, Mr. Francis, told me that I would have to take a ferry to New Jersey in the morning. The market, he said, opened at ten o'clock and there was some business for me to transact. Little did he know what other business I had in mind.

I was there well before ten the next morning and I bought the certificates for $3,150. I returned to my office where I promptly wired General Obregon that I would be at the Santa Rita Hotel in Nogales on the Arizona-Sonora border on Monday and wished to meet with him. It was now Thursday, which meant I was going to have to leave New York by train on Friday in order to make it via Tucson, Arizona. To Nogales and back with sufficient cash for exigencies was going to leave damn little cash in my bank account, but no matter. I was willing to risk all. At that point I recall looking out my office window down into the street and hoping I had made the right decision. Finally I started to plot and plan. I would sell the certificates to the Mexican government, using the general as intermediary, for a fortune. How big a fortune? I had no idea. I would, as they say, play it by ear. The thought suddenly occurred to me that I didn't even have a lawyer or know a soul in Arizona. I stole another look at the men hurrying along Wall Street. I'd seen the Yaqui Valley. They hadn't. I knew the general, or at least I thought I knew him, and well—I was going to risk it. And having arrived at this firm decision, I left my office at five in high spirits. Up to now, I reminded myself, I had been merely studying the art of making a business deal. Now I was about to have my first practical experience, and on a high level too, with the governor of the state of Sonora, Mexico.

We traveled by train in those days, and the service was good and the food excellent. I spent most of my trip in the club car, reading and watching the scenery. I got off at Tucson, hired a car, and drove directly to Nogales for my rendezvous with the general. Waiting for me at the small hotel was a note asking me to meet him across the border at eight o'clock that evening. It advised that his military aide would join me at the customs and escort me to the rendezvous.

After a short siesta, I donned my only navy blue suit and walked the short distance to the border. Lively music played by a mariachi band spilled out as I passed a bar. Exactly as planned, the general's heavily mustachioed aide joined me at the customs and together we zigzagged through the dark, narrow streets, finally stopping before a handsome house. We entered, climbed one flight of stairs, stopped before a large barricaded door which my guide flung open, saying, with a deep bow, "*Por favor, passe usted.*" I stepped inside and stood for a moment, blinking in surprise. I hadn't known what to expect, but certainly this big-business-deal setting was as far afield from the Wall Street norm as you could get.

The room was so small that the table, around which some five or six Mexicans sat in native costume, almost touched the four walls. The men were playing poker, and chips and gold coins littered the table top. Curls of cigar smoke floated in the air that was spiced with the pungent scent of tequila. I recognized General Obregon, who rose to greet me in Spanish. Then one of the other men stepped forward and, in good English, said that he would act as interpreter for the general's knowledge of English was limited. He pulled up a chair for me on the general's left and then settled himself in another one nearby.

A very stilted attempt at conversation followed. I felt hopelessly out of control of the situation, and felt that my formal blue suit was not in harmony with the surroundings. This went on for some fifteen or twenty minutes, when suddenly the general burst out laughing and said, through his interpreter, "This reminds me of the problem of the young girls today. No matter how long their stockings or how short their skirts, they never seem to meet." There was a split second of silence and then everyone in the room exploded with delight. A round of tequila was proposed to the girls, and the ice was broken.

"And now tell me what really is your serious business, Mr. Whitney," said the general through his interpreter.

Firmly gripping the tequila glass in an attempt to appear more poised, I said, "I have acquired a one-third interest in the Richardson Construction Company and I'm here to see if your government might wish to buy it."

The general wasted no time. He replied at once and his interpreter said: "It is quite possible. Do you have a lawyer, Mr. Whitney?"

"Unfortunately, I don't," I said. "Can you recommend one?"

"I have an American lawyer in Nogales," replied the general. "If you wish, Mr. Whitney, I will be agreeable that he represent both of us."

In the silence which followed I admit that I didn't know if this would be good or bad for me. Instinct, I guess, prompted me to say, "I accept your kind offer, General. Can we meet tomorrow morning?"

The general paused to take a long puff on his cigar before answering. "We will meet here at nine o'clock if this is agreeable to you, señor Whitney."

"I shall be here," I said with all the control I could put into my voice.

I was at the next day's rendezvous promptly at nine, to be greeted by a clean-cut young American who introduced himself as my lawyer-to-be. He was very businesslike. The room so cluttered the previous evening was spic and span now. He told me that he was thoroughly familiar with the affairs of the Richardson Construction Company. "If you let me do the negotiating," he said, "I believe I can get you a half million dollars for your certificates. Would this be satisfactory, Mr. Whitney?"

I gulped and pretended to be considering the matter. Then I rose to my feet and said, "Yes, but I'll need some cash down and large monthly payments thereafter."

The young lawyer nodded. "Let's proceed then with the meeting. General Obregon is a busy man and also a man of few words." He excused himself and returned a few minutes later, accompanied by the general, who was in a very cheerful mood. No sooner had he made his entrance than a Mexican boy placed coffee and doughnuts on the table and withdrew, leaving the three of us alone.

Our meeting lasted no more than fifteen minutes. I accepted half a million for my certificates and it was further agreed that I be paid fifty thousand American dollars a month for ten months with interest fixed at six percent. After which the general and I celebrated our deal with a round of margaritas. Then looking me squarely in the eye, he wished me a safe journey home, an early return to his beloved Mexico, and with that he took his departure. I sat there with my lawyer, an empty coffee cup, a half-eaten doughnut, and a feeling of exhilaration hard to describe.

That was the high peak that started my business career. A half-million dollars is a big sum at any time, but to a man in his twenties it was staggering. Most important, however, is the fact that with this windfall I founded Pan American Airways. The following year, by selling some stock in Pan Am, I founded the Hudson Bay Mining and Smelting Company, and then five years later, by selling some of its stock I founded Marineland near St. Augustine, Florida. I was on my way.

My wise father, the well known Harry Payne Whitney, never knew that it was his only son, nicknamed Sonny, who bought those "worthless certificates" for $3,150.

4 | No More Regrets

IT SEEMS incredible since, in a manner of speaking, I had been brought up with horses, that I didn't see a horse race until I had been out of college for several years—1927, to be exact. Well, at least it was a big race —the best there is, the Kentucky Derby—and I arrived in style from New York in my father's private Pullman car, the "Wanderer." I recall, however, that I wasn't overly impressed with my first sight of the Commonwealth of Kentucky, now one of my favorite spots in the world.

"We're here, Mister Sonny," said Randolph, my father's black butler, as the train pulled to a stop in what, to me at least, appeared to be the middle of nowhere. "Step out and look around," he suggested, and I did just that, observing from the back observation platform of the "Wanderer" the lush green fields and high-spreading trees.

"Where are we?" I asked.

"In the middle of your father's farm and what you all sees there is blue grass."

"But it isn't blue," I said.

"It will be soon when it goes to seed," Randolph assured me. "The flower is blue. You'll see, Mister Sonny." And being a dyed-in-the-wool optimist, Randolph went on to assure me that my father's entry, Whiskery, was sure to win the Derby. "He's by Whiskbroom out of that great mare Prudery," he said. "He can't lose."

"If you say so, Randolph, I believe you," I said respectfully. It was just so much Greek to me. Randolph flashed me one of his happiest grins and then he suggested I'd best start breakfast since it was a long way to Churchill Downs and he figured father and his cronies, who were aboard too, would want to start rolling again.

Breakfast was being served in the large combination sitting room and dining room. My father and his two friends, whose names I don't recall now, were already seated so I took the empty chair. And no sooner did I sit down than Papa let me in on his surprise.

"Sonny," he said, looking very regal in his Chinese dressing gown, "you'll be going to the Derby alone. I get too nervous." He put down the spoon with which he'd been scooping the soft-boiled egg from its shell, and reached down into the pocket of his dressing gown. "Here are your box tickets, and Buck will drive you." I took the tickets from him and waited for further instructions. "If Whiskery wins," he continued, returning his attention to the egg, "you'll have to go to the winner's circle and make a speech. Now," he smiled, "eat up because you have a three-hour drive ahead of you."

And eat I did. Fruit. Eggs with country ham, grits and gravy. Hot biscuits dripping with honey. My first introduction to a real southern meal. And while I was stuffing myself, the conversation at the table turned to horse talk. I was out of my depth, of course, but I did take note of the frequent mention of a horse apparently named Regret. Papa was saying that he would challenge any man to walk down the row of stalls and pick

Regret out only seeing her head and neck. There was nothing feminine about Regret's head and neck, he said with no little satisfaction. "That's the reason I believe that she beat the colts in the Derby," he said. "I don't believe a feminine-looking girl can beat the men in sports that require brute strength and endurance." He paused to let that thought register. His two friends nodded in agreement. "I'll be interested to see what kind of a foal she produces this year," continued Papa. "She's had nothing outstanding yet."

One of Papa's friends allowed that he'd very much like to see Regret. She was, after all, the only filly ever to win the Derby. Papa said that he would arrange for them to go over to his farm and see all the mares, foals and yearlings. For a moment, as I watched him sitting there so enthusiastically talking horses with his cronies, I suspected he had all but forgotten I was there. But no, just as I was reaching for still another hot biscuit, he turned to me and said, "Sonny, you'd better get dressed. Here's one hundred dollars for your lunch—and you might want to make a bet."

"Thank you, Papa," I said, grabbing the biscuit and the hundred-dollar bill. "I'm on my way." And off I went to dress, stuffing the money in my pocket, rather amused that my father still didn't know that I was already a person of considerable wealth.

When I returned, Randolph told me that Buck and a Packard car were on the road waiting for me. I jumped in beside Buck and off we went over a one-lane dirt track through father's farm. We crossed a fast-flowing creek that Buck told me was the Elkhorn, and he said it was full of fish. Soon we emerged onto a macadam highway, and from there along a string of winding roads that took us through several small villages, until we reached the famous city of Louisville. Then, finally, we arrived at Churchill Downs and joined the hundreds of people streaming toward the racetrack.

I had no trouble finding my father's box. But it was empty, so I thought I'd look around for a place to eat. Apparently I was continually hungry in those days. I ended up in a crowded lunchroom at a table with three strangers. After a moment one of them introduced himself. "I'm Ring Lardner," he said, extending his hand. "Please join us."

"I'm Sonny Whitney," I replied. "Thank you."

"Are you Harry Payne's son?" he said. I nodded. And then he tipped back in his chair and looked me over. "I believe Whiskery is going to win," he said, breaking the silence at the table. "Here's luck!" and he hoisted a tall glass.

I ordered lunch plus a Scotch and soda, and proceeded to try and hold my own in the conversation around the table. Since I was Harry Payne Whitney's son, the men assumed I knew all about racetrack matters and I put up the best bluff I could.

Two—or was it three?—Scotches later, I was telling Mr. Lardner about my father's instructions. If Whiskery won the Derby, I was to accept the trophy and make a speech. "What the hell do I say and where do I go?" I asked, no longer pretending to know what it was all about.

Ring Lardner grinned. And taking a pencil from his pocket, he said, "Here, Sonny, let me write something on your shirt cuff." Obligingly, I shot my cuff out from under my jacket and waited. He turned to our waiter and inquired, "How would you describe the track, Hatch?" Hatch replied, "Muddy, Mr. Lardner." "Okay, I have it!" exclaimed Lardner. "He won because his mudder was a mudder." Grabbing my arm, he proceeded to write that on my cuff while everyone guffawed.

Finishing with considerable flourish, Lardner put down his pen and said, "Now, Son, you better get on up there because it's about race time. We'll pay your check. You've hardly time to make a bet."

"Many thanks," I mumbled, getting to my feet and sprinting off in the direction of the track.

The crowd by this time was so thick that I could hardly move. It was sheer bedlam. Bands playing. Glasses clinking. People shouting. Furthermore, I was more than a trifle confused after those Scotch and sodas. I climbed up and down the rickety stairways of the old wooden grandstand and got completely lost. Then I heard a roar go up from the throng and suddenly everyone seemed to be jumping up and down. When the shouting subsided, a man close to me grabbed my arm and blasted my ear with "I told you he'd win. Whiskery! I have the winning ticket. He's my horse—the *winner!*" And with that he turned and raced up the stairs to cash in his ticket.

I was stunned. It wasn't possible. Or was it? *It was.* I had missed the race. "Where is the winner's circle?" I asked the person next to me. "Out there," he said, waving his arms wildly.

I started off in the general direction in which I thought he had waved, and found everybody else appeared to be determined to move in the opposite direction. So finally I decided to join them rather than fight them. And where do you suppose I landed about twenty minutes later? At the entrance gates, where at the sight of me Buck rushed up and grabbed my arm. "I told you he'd win, Mister Sonny," he exclaimed. "Now let's get out of here quick or we never will." He steered me to the car, gently shoved me inside, and off we drove. I had a headache and closed my eyes, resting my head on the back of the seat. What was my father going to say? I hadn't collected the trophy. I hadn't made a speech. I hadn't even seen the race.

I must have dozed off because suddenly, or so it seemed to me, we were pulling up alongside Papa's Pullman car. It was ablaze with lights, and I could see my father and three men sitting around a card table with stacks of poker chips in front of them. I clambered up out of the car and headed for what I was certain was going to be a showdown with my father.

As I stepped inside he looked up and demanded, "Did you have a good day, Sonny?" Fortunately, he didn't wait for a reply. "Randolph has dinner waiting for you," he said, reaching out for some chips. "I suggest you eat and then take a walk around the farm. Randolph tells me there'll be a celebration tonight. You might want to see it."

"Did you make a bet, Sonny?" one of his cronies asked me. I couldn't lie. "I was so excited I forgot all about it," I stammered, adding, "some men paid for my lunch." The hundred-dollar bill was still in my pocket.

Miraculously, I thought at the time, there were no more questions so I left them to their poker game and went off for another delicious southern meal of fried chicken, corn pudding, and fresh greens, followed by warm apple pie.

Just as I was finishing the pie, Buck emerged from the dark shadows outside the Pullman. "Come with me, Mister Sonny," he said. "You got nothin' else to do." He was perfectly correct, of course, and so I followed him off down the railroad track in the silver light of a rising moon. My stomach full and my headache gone, I happily followed Buck for about a mile, until he turned off the tracks and led the way down a wide footpath. Then we crossed the Elkhorn creek on a footbridge and emerged onto a large and level pasture. There Buck stopped and announced with pride, "Look, Mister Sonny, there they is."

On the far side of the pasture a hill rose against the moonlight and on top of that hill there was a bright bonfire burning. "I'll lead you. Come on," whispered Buck.

As we climbed the hill, voices raised in song rolled down toward us. When we reached the top, I simply stood there spellbound. For there was a horse standing silhouetted against the light of the bonfire and dozens of black people were crowded around it, singing.

"That's Regret," whispered Buck, "and they're singing our local songs in her praise. And now we've raised Whiskery on this farm, another great winner of the Derby." Then we proceeded to walk slowly in the direction of the horse until we were soon lost in the crowd. I had never before heard the local songs. I found their harmony and semireligious overtones truly exciting. This was a part of horse racing too, a side most people rarely heard or read about.

"This will go on all night," Buck said. "I think I'd

best take you home and then come back myself." And with that we crept stealthily back into the shadows and followed the long trail back to the "Wanderer."

I never came back to Kentucky until after my father died three years later. In his will he left the racing stable to be sold. I had no intention of buying it, but I did. Was it the nostalgic memory of my first visit to Kentucky that impelled me to buy it? It is true that I have had no Regrets, nor even a Whiskery, but there is always hope, and that is what has kept me in the horse business to this very year 1977. I have won many stakes classics but never the Kentucky Derby, which is the race every owner dreams about winning.

5 | The Chocolate Soldier

I HAVE HAD some thrilling experiences with my race-horses and perhaps the most exciting of my equestrian superstars was Equipoise. Because of his rich brown coat, he was known as the Chocolate Soldier.

He wasn't a big horse but he had tremendous courage. Handicapped with one badly formed foot which often caused him excruciating pain, he nevertheless gave everything that was in him to win a race. Several times, in fact, he was disqualified for biting another horse in the neck when trying to pass him. Even my first meeting with Equipoise was dramatic. My dear father died in 1930, only a week before the running of the Pimlico Futurity, one of the classic races for two-year-olds. That year there were three standout colts: Twenty Grand, Mate, Equipoise. The experts differed on which was the best. This race would settle it.

But I wasn't at all certain I should run him so soon after my father's funeral. William Woodward, chairman of The Jockey Club and a very close friend of father's, phoned me and urged me to go ahead. He said my father would approve. "Please run him," he said.

So run him I did. Ordinarily, it would have been a happy occasion. This was the first horse to run in my name. So I traveled to Baltimore dressed in a mourning suit with a bowler hat, and with mixed emotions. But before long Equipoise had me jumping to my feet and shouting. Left behind at the post by some twenty lengths, he slowly wore his field down and then won by one-half length.

Equipoise was on his way to becoming the king of the horse world. Little did I dream at the time that a few years later, this marvelous animal would be responsible for bringing me face-to-face with Al Capone, king of the underworld.

It began not with the notorious Al, however, but with his brother who phoned my New York office one day and asked to speak to me. I knew that he owned an important racetrack in the Chicago area and, curiosity aroused, I told my secretary I would accept the call.

He was a well-spoken man and wasted no time getting to the reason for his call: he offered to put up $25,000 and a gold trophy if I would send Equipoise to his track for a match race against Gallant Sir, the pride of the Midwest. Gallant Sir hadn't been defeated in eleven starts. It was a most interesting offer, and Capone and I agreed that a mile and a quarter—the same distance as the Kentucky Derby—would be appropriate. I proposed an open race instead of only the two horses. Capone agreed, and we promptly settled on a race to be called the Hawthorne Gold Cup.

Then I called my trainer, Tom Healey, and told him the deal. He was pleased and, although Equipoise's foot was giving him trouble, Tom thought it would heal sufficiently for him to be ready to run. Then, only the day before the race, Tom called to say that the foot was worse and that he would prefer not to run Equipoise.

Would it be dangerous to the horse's future if he were to run?

"No more than it has been once or twice before," Tom said. Did he think he could run his best under the circumstances? "On his courage alone, yes," he replied without hesitation. So I decided then and there to go ahead with the race. There had been so much publicity about it, I knew that if I were to scratch Equipoise, the press and public would very likely think we were afraid of being beaten.

Equipoise gave one of his most valiant performances, winning the race after having fought off one particular horse in the backstretch who kept bumping into him. Equipoise left his tormentor behind, hooked up with Gallant Sir and, in a battle of champions, pulled away in the last one-eighth mile to win. As I made my way to the winner's circle, I saw Capone and he nodded, smiled, and that was that. And I rather imagined that was going to be my last encounter with the brothers Capone.

But the next winter while exploring the waters around Nassau in the Bahamas on my fifty-foot ketch "Adventure," I joined some friends ashore at the Bahamian Club for a game of poker and heard the rumor that Al Capone was in hiding somewhere on the island. Nobody had seen him and nobody planned to track down the rumor to test its authenticity. Capone's reputation was a chilling one. I particularly remembered the story of his killing a rival by repeatedly stabbing him in the face with an ice pick. Having had one peaceful contact with his brother was quite enough Capone family for me.

At about 1:00 A.M., while concentrating on the card game, I felt a tap on my shoulder. I looked up at a youngish man who promptly bent down to whisper in my ear, "The boss would like to see you. Follow me." It sounded more like a command than an invitation.

The fellow simply moved across the room, confident that I would do the sensible thing and follow him. I flagged an attentive waiter and asked him if he knew the fellow. He too bent down to whisper in my ear. "One of Capone's crew," he said. Now it was my turn to whisper. "Is his boss really at the Club?" The waiter said he was indeed, "in one of the back rooms."

Why would Al Capone want to see me? Had I asked them, none of my friends at the card table would have had the answer. Neither would the waiter, who was even now moving very cautiously away from our table.

I felt my curiosity getting the edge over my common sense. Anyway, I figured Capone wouldn't— couldn't—harm me in a well known place like the Bahamian Club. So I got up and joined Capone's man, following him out a side door, down several corridors, and finally into a room which looked like a private dining room. There at the table sat Al Capone, a bodyguard standing close behind him. His black hair neatly combed, his rather considerable bulk encased in a striped silk shirt, he certainly didn't look fierce.

Capone got to his feet, shot out his chubby hand and shook mine with a very firm grip. He actually smiled as he invited me to sit down. He seemed extremely low-key, almost gentle. Close up, I thought he seemed like a sorely tired, overweight barber on a much-needed holiday. A barber who, judging by the champagne and canapés, was denying himself nothing. Would I like some champagne? Indeed I would, my mouth being uncommonly dry. I no sooner had said yes than his bodyguard, a slight fellow with a gun strapped to his thigh, was pouring me a tumblerfull.

His thick forefinger sporting a flashy diamond, Capone sat there watching me drain the glass, his hand slowly tapping the table top. Then he struck up convivial conversation. He said he liked Nassau very much. Its climate. Its beaches. Its friendly people. I found myself agreeing with everything. I actually *did* enjoy Nassau's climate, beaches, and friendly people, but had I not, I doubt that I would have made an issue of it. Then, reaching over and plucking a canapé from the tray on the table, the undisputed king of the underworld abruptly switched to a new topic—*horses.*

"Mr. Whitney," he began, wiping his fingers on a napkin and then patting it against his lips, "you know that I love horses. I race some of my own. And I happen to particularly admire your stable, and when I heard that you were in the Club, I wanted to meet you." At this point he smiled and it was an extremely pleasant smile. "I hope you'll excuse the way I had to invite you," he continued, "but it—well, it wouldn't be wise for me to be seen inside the Club. I don't fix the gambling here," he said—almost apologetically, I thought—"but some people might think that I do and if they saw me here, the Club might lose some customers."

"I understand," I said. "I was only curious to know why you wanted to talk to me."

His expression became extremely serious. "You've produced some great horses, but none greater than Equipoise," he said. "And I asked you here, Mr. Whitney, to apologize to you for something I did. My conscience will never be free until I do." He paused, seeming uncertain how to proceed. I actually felt myself wanting to help out. "Was it in Chicago, in the Hawthorne Gold Cup?" I prompted.

"Yes sir, it was. I'm sure you remember that horse who was trying to bump Equipoise into the rail on the backstretch." I nodded. "That was my horse," he said, "and the jockey was acting under my instructions. I had a big bet on Gallant Sir."

Although I had suspected as much at the time, I was now surprised to hear it confirmed. Capone went on as though once he had gotten the courage to confess, he wanted to get it all over with. "I did an injustice to your truly great horse, Mr. Whitney. I don't expect you to forgive me."

Well, now he'd said it and his conscience was free at last. He really seemed relieved. "Now that I've told you, I'd like to invite you to be my guest in Miami next month at the Sharkey championship fight."

With such poise as I could muster, I told Al Capone that I wouldn't be able to accept his kind invitation. I explained that I was starting out the next month on an extended trip through Latin America on behalf of Pan American Airways. In a moment the same man who had escorted me to this rendezvous was standing beside me, ready to lead me back to the main gambling room. Al Capone stood up and we shook hands and I left the room feeling much more relaxed than I had when I entered.

I never saw Capone again. He died a normal death not too many years later. And I suppose it sounds trite, but he had taught me something I think rather important: no man is completely evil. This one, often called one of the most evil men who ever lived, had apologized for having once tried to harm an animal.

6 | Gone with the Wind

THE 1930s were extremely busy years in my life. I was chairman of the board of directors of three major pioneering ventures, each of which I had founded: Pan American Airways, Hudson Bay Mining and Smelting Company, and Marineland of Florida.

I was now also busy with things artistic. I was a director of the Metropolitan Opera Company of New York, as well as a trustee of the American Museum of Natural History. And since I've always had more than a fair share of energy and stamina, I also found time to organize and captain the Old Westbury polo team which won the championship of the United States. I suppose, according to life insurance standards, I was in the prime of my life, although I believe a healthy, active individual is always in the prime of life no matter what his age. There I was in my thirties, enjoying an active life and, as usual, looking around for a challenge or two as well. And, as usual, I eventually found one or, to be more exact, *two*.

First, I took a plunge into politics. I ran for Congress of the United States on the Democratic ticket from the First Congressional District of Long Island, New York, and was defeated. It was the only unsuccessful one of all my projects of this period. And I suppose it made me more eager than ever for a challenge in another field. Little did I dream that I would find it in, of all things, motion pictures, where I would be involved in the making of one of the most famous and successful films in the history of the cinema.

It came about this way. One of my closest friends at that time was Merian Cooper, one of the pioneers in the making of outdoor adventure films. *King Kong* was one of his most recent successes, and now he wanted to form a company to make films of classic dimensions—films that would also pioneer in the use of color, which was just being perfected. He asked me if I would head up such a company.

I was intrigued, of course, but I had to tell him that I simply didn't have the time to direct such a company. Still, it was too exciting an opportunity to pass up and I told him that I would talk to my cousin, Jock Whitney, and see if perhaps I could enlist him. I didn't tell Merian (didn't want to give him false hopes) but I strongly suspected it wouldn't be too difficult to get Jock enthusiastic and it wasn't. He agreed to head up Merian's proposed production company; he would be president and the two Whitney families would participate fifty-fifty in the financing. So Selznick International was born with the talented young David Selznick as our producer, and off we went turning out one hit after the other, most of them in what was soon being referred to in the industry as "glorious" Technicolor: *Rebecca, A Star Is Born,* and *Becky Sharp.* They were good box-office successes and yet we not only didn't make a profit but found ourselves several million dollars in the red. Selznick was such a perfectionist that our production budgets were monumental. We simply had to come up with a blockbuster if Selznick International was to survive. And we were determined to survive; *quit* was a word missing from our corporate vocabulary.

So the hunt was on for a super script from which we could make a super motion picture. It was the year 1936, and one day Kay Brown, a very clever young lady who worked in our New York office, concluded that she had found one and she sent off the following wire to Dave Selznick in Hollywood: "Have a great manuscript. The story is laid in the South during the Civil War period. The primary theme is the love story between a strong man and a strong girl. The secondary theme is the intense love this girl had for her land and home. The manuscript is very long. Believe I can buy it from the author, Margaret Mitchell, for under $50,000. Please wire instructions."

Selznick read the manuscript and was most enthusiastic. He called a meeting with Jock and me, transmitted his enthusiasm to us and we agreed to purchase the manuscript without further delay. But a little later, Selznick, anxious as he was to direct the film version of this as-yet-unpublished novel, said he would do so only on the following conditions: (1) that we adhere faithfully to the novel, (2) that the production cost be in the neighborhood of four million dollars (a huge sum for those days), (3) that the ultimate production play for approximately four hours, and (4) that no actor other than Clark Gable be cast in the role of Rhett Butler. He allowed that getting the right actress to portray Scarlett O'Hara would be a challenge. By this time Jock and I had read the manuscript too, and our enthusiasm knew no bounds. If anything less than wholly enthusiastic, we might not have agreed to Selznick's terms, because here we were once again about to produce another staggeringly expensive motion picture, one that would run for four hours before the fadeout. We were really sticking our necks out. But Selznick was adamant on his terms, and after two hours of intense discussion, Jock and I wholeheartedly agreed to proceed with the production of *Gone with the Wind*.

While the script was still being written, the novel was published and became a best seller. Not only did David Selznick insist that Clark Gable play Rhett Butler; we were besieged with letters from the public *demanding* that we cast Gable in the part. Again, as Selznick had predicted, casting the role of Scarlett O'Hara was much more difficult. Letters poured in; it seems every third or fourth person who read the novel could see a favorite actress in the role, but there were no overwhelming favorites.

As the novel became even more popular and the public more passionate about who should portray Scarlett on the screen, Selznick called a meeting and said that it was his considered opinion that we should find an unknown and try to make her our star. We agreed that it seemed like a perfect solution to a dilemma, so the search for Scarlett O'Hara was off and running. It was not a publicity stunt as some people may have suspected at the time. There was already so much interest in our upcoming film version of the novel that we had no need for further publicity. We were honestly eager to find an unknown to play the part, for we knew that were we to choose an established actress, no matter how supremely talented she was, a goodly portion of the public would be disappointed that we hadn't chosen another. So a talented, young unknown seemed a very intelligent solution.

Applicants popped up from all parts of the United

States. We gave many of them screen tests. Then one day came the ideal Scarlett O'Hara. She was young, beautiful, and she could act. Furthermore, almost unbelievably, she had an authentic southern accent. She was from New Orleans.

Now perhaps you never heard of the censorship bureau known as the Will Hayes Office. In the 1930s no motion picture could be produced until the Hayes Office approved both cast and script. By the time our Scarlett from New Orleans turned up, the other major and minor parts in the story had been cast and approved by Hayes. Then came the blow: the Will Hayes Office informed us that we couldn't sign her. They had researched her background and found that her grandmother had Negro blood. There was no arguing her case. The decision was final. Now, over thirty-five years later, how different it would be. If the issue were raised at all, today we would be applauded for selecting her.

I am ashamed to say I don't recall exactly how David Selznick found Vivien Leigh. She was known in England but virtually unknown to American movie audiences. And, of course, the very idea of a British girl playing Scarlett O'Hara, who by now had become an American heroine to millions of Americans, was very daring indeed. Miss Leigh looked the part, however, even to possessing Scarlett's green eyes. In fact, she had all the requirements for the part except the southern accent. So with complete faith in Selznick's selection, we sent her to a speech teacher to transfer her accent from Mayfair to south of the Mason-Dixon line. She was a smart girl and did it in six weeks.

To Vivien Leigh's everlasting credit it is difficult

now to believe that anyone could have been a more believable Scarlett. She loved the part and she lived the part. She was Scarlett O'Hara. And happily, the Will Hayes Office approved!

Then we heard from the Will Hayes Office once again. What now? Well, I'm sure you remember Rhett Butler's final exit line—one of the most famous lines in movie history—as he walks out of the house vowing never to return. Scarlett has tried her best to dissuade him but he replies, "Frankly, my dear, I don't give a damn." Scarlett isn't too distressed; she looks to tomorrow to solve her problems. But the Will Hayes Office was disturbed. Hayes said we couldn't use the word *damn*. It was profane. *Darn* was okay, but not *damn*.

We presented a carefully thought out case to them: *Gone with the Wind* was already an American classic, and the line in question was in common usage. Would they change the language in a Shakespeare play? And certainly the Bard used some rougher language than *damn*. Margaret Mitchell was a southern lady herself and she used the word *damn*. Rhett himself certainly would have used the word; it was in keeping with his character. In fact, we argued, it would be out of character for him to say *darn*. After several weeks of argument, logic prevailed and we won.

The grand opening in New York City projected our eagerly awaited film before the most critical and sophisticated audience in the United States. Critics had raved over the story in book form. They were going to be super-critical of the film version. We felt safe with Clark Gable, seemingly everybody's choice for Rhett Butler. But what about Vivien Leigh as Scarlett? Olivia deHaviland as Melanie? Leslie Howard as Ashley? And would an audience sit through the four hours required by the film? There were few movies, if any, which took more than two. Would an audience accept the final scene which left Rhett and Scarlett's future in limbo? With the major theme a love story, mightn't they expect the movie to end with a discreet love scene? The film had been well received in Atlanta. Would it play in New York? Being a practical as well as artistic person, I thought of my investment. The survival of Selznick International now depended entirely on the success of *Gone with the Wind.*

At intermission time, I struggled through the crowd to mingle in the lobby and in the street with the audience. I was delighted with what I heard. They were ecstatic about the picture. The bell rang and some of New York's greatest sophisticates stubbed out their cigarettes to rush back inside the theatre and regain their seats. When the music started and the lights dimmed, there was wild, spontaneous applause.

With the final scene, the theatre was once again flooded with light and a roar of approval went up from the audience. No doubt about it, we had scored a great triumph. And though I was fairly bursting with pride (and great relief), I did my best to behave according to Kipling: "If you can meet with triumph and disaster / And treat those two imposters just the same." I was learning that when I had a triumph I should not boast too much and when a disaster, not cry for sympathy.

I must admit that today I boast more about my role in producing *Gone with the Wind* than I did then, for it is not generally known that I was involved, as Selznick took most of the publicity. And finally, my wife, Mary, and our children go to see it every time it comes to town, so that it has become just as great a high peak to them as it was to me. Thanks to the enduring magic of film, this is a high peak we can share together.

7 | Tournasol

POLO WAS in its heyday in the 1930s. When my father captained the first great American team to defeat the British in 1909, America became more polo-conscious than ever before. Then when my boyhood pal Tommy Hitchcock changed the game from one of tactical skill to one of speed, long hitting, and rough riding, polo became even more popular. So by the time the 1930s rolled around, well-bred ponies were bringing astronomical prices if they had the speed and endurance required on the polo field. To mount and train a championship team in those days required as much thought and skill as it does to train and ride a Secretariat today.

I was actually a mediocre and not a serious player until I got the great urge to overthrow my cousin Jock Whitney's champion Greentree team. Jock and his fellow players Tommy Hitchcock, Gerald Balding, and Pete Bostwick were held almost in awe by the polo-playing world. I felt an urge to compete every time I read about them in the press or met with them socially, for we were all good friends. Gradually I found myself no longer content with being a mediocre player. Competition always spurs me on and the thought of challenging the invincible Greentree team kept recurring. Soon I swung into action.

I wasted no time in recruiting a potentially strong team: Michael Phipps, Cecil Smith, and Stewart Iglehart. So now cousin Jock, my *Gone with the Wind* partner (we'd just bought the film rights to the novel that year), was my adversary. I wisely went to work to improve my game. My father had, after all, beaten the unbeatable British. I was going to beat this team of unbeatable Americans. The problem was that while my teammates were all well established high-goal players and had therefore a fair claim to fame, I was the weak link. I was going to have to remedy that.

First, I recruited Charlie Jones, an ex-prizefighter who was my bodyguard during my campaign for Congress, to condition me. Polo at Meadowbrook started each year in the spring, and the open championship was not until late September, which gave me some five months to participate actively in the game. So I fixed up an old polo field near my Long Island home, hired Ivor Balding, the brother of Gerald Balding who was on Jock's team, to condition the ponies, and I was out practicing every evening after work. All that spring I practiced, and then in mid-July I went to Whitney Park in the Adirondacks where, with Charlie Jones, I made a boxing ring out of a tent platform. Every day I went a full six rounds with Charlie, skipped rope for one half-hour, and rowed a guide boat at a good clip for three to four miles. I was like a pugilist preparing for a championship match. When I finally returned to Long Island to join in the pre-tournament games, I was in excellent shape mentally and physically. I had absolutely no qualms about competing for the open championship, despite the fact that Jock's Greentree team was still the overwhelming favorite.

The final two weeks before the open championship were spent in practice games and selecting the most suitable ponies for each member of my team. A game of polo consisted of eight ten-minute periods of play with short intermissions to change ponies. A strong pony could be played in two periods, no more.

On the day of the open championship tournament, the grandstands at Meadowbrook, which could seat some 20,000 spectators, were strained to capacity for the three-hundred yard length of the championship polo field.

My new Old Westbury team rose to the occasion, and after eliminating two competitors we reached the finals in full swing. And by the time we came to the finals, the sportswriters were in agreement that if we could maintain our high standard of teamwork and hitting, and if I could improve my handicap rating to at least six goals, we could give Greentree a battle.

On the day of the finals, I lined up my team with Phipps at 1, Smith 2, Iglehart 3, and myself back. Greentree lined up Bostwick 1, Balding 2, Hitchcock 3, and cousin Jock back. This of course pitted me against Pete Bostwick, the greatest goal shooter of the year, a crack steeplechase rider, and mounted on top-speed ponies. Well aware of Pete's deadly accuracy, I figured I had better cover him closely at all times. In other words, never let him get a free run with the ball. The back's position, you see, is a defensive one, chiefly concerned with protecting his goal. My teammates were keyed to a high pitch. We had confidence in each other and were out to win.

I chose Tournasol, the great Argentine-bred pony, for the first period as I planned to rough Pete Bostwick from the start. Tournasol had no fear whatsoever; he would charge full speed into anything that you pointed him at.

Still the game seesawed back and forth for six periods with neither side getting more than a one-goal lead. Then came the accident, with me the victim. Jock and I were engaged in a battle to reach the ball when he swung his mallet across his pony's forelegs to make a cross shot. I was leaning far out of my saddle, and the head of his mallet gave me a resounding crack over the right eye. The next thing I remember was lying flat on my back on the grass, with Dr. Bob Miller leaning over me. My head was wrapped in a bandage.

Once Bob saw me open my eyes, he got right to the point. "Sonny," he whispered, "you have a severe deep cut over your right eye. I know how much this game means to you. If you say the word, I'll sew it up and give permission for you to play it out."

I got right to the point, too. "Do it," I said.

So time out was called for just twenty minutes, during which time I was rushed to the emergency tent on the sidelines and then stitches were taken without anesthetic. And I was back in the game. The scar is still there today to remind me.

At the end of eight periods the game was tied, and the referee announced there would be an extra sudden-death period. Whichever team made the first goal would win the game and the open championship. The two captains, Jock and yours truly, agreed to a fifteen-minute rest period before resuming the all-important play.

I slid off my great mare, Fuss Budget, and Ivor Balding greeted me. "Are you okay, Sonny?" I nodded. "What do you want to ride this time?" "Tournasol!" I replied, without a minute's hesitation, for I knew our only hope was that I stop Pete Bostwick from making that winning goal. But I also realized that I had already ridden Tournasol two hard periods. "Do you think he can do it?" I asked Ivor.

"I guarantee he'll be ready," Ivor said.

When the bell rang, Old Westbury rode out on the field, all four of us united by the offensive spirit. When we reached the center field, Greentree had not yet arrived. At the sight of us, a roar went up from the grandstands. We had a huddle and I, astride Tournasol, told my teammates to "play offensive all the way out—it's the only way we can win."

That extra sudden-death period was a battle, with both teams on the offensive and eight men and eight magnificent ponies giving it all they had. We were deadlocked for five minutes, and then came our break.

The ball was mid-field with Hitchcock and Smith locked in a mad, bumping brawl to get to it. In the split second before they reached it, I saw that Hitchcock was going to win. So I turned Tournasol sharply inside Pete and went all out for the goalposts. Hitchcock's near-side backhand sent the ball sailing over my head on a beeline to the goalposts, and there—three lengths ahead of me—rode Gerald Balding. If he reached that ball, he would only have to tap it through the posts and win the game and glory. And he knew it. Looking over his right shoulder, he shouted back to me, "You'll never catch me now!"

My response was to dig both spurs into Tournasol, and that gallant animal promptly poured it on. I caught Gerald just before he got to the ball only a few yards from the goalposts, bumped him off it, and I was just able to slice a backhand shot away from the posts. It was a short shot, and Iglehart, judging it correctly, lifted a long backhand across the field toward our goal. Smith, who a moment before was about to lose to Hitchcock, had anticipated the shot and was wide-open in pursuit. He reached the ball ahead of Hitchcock and smacked one under his pony's neck and on up the field. It was to the left of the posts but Mike Phipps was there, dribbled it once and then tapped it through for the winning goal.

Mike scored the winning goal, but the real hero in my book was Tournasol, that tough little Argentine pony who had caught Gerald Balding and then bumped him so hard that he couldn't make the winning shot for goal.

"How did he do it?" I asked Ivor Balding as soon as I dismounted.

Ivor flashed a smile. "I poured a quart of Johnnie Walker whiskey down his throat," he said. "Wouldn't that have made you frisky?"

"It sure would," I muttered, remembering for the first time since my accident that I had a painful gash over my right eye. "I need a jiggerful right now."

After this victory I sold all my ponies at public auction and never played polo again. Having won the open championship I had achieved my goal. But who do you suppose bought that great pony, Tournasol? Pete Bostwick, of course. He had been roughed up too many times by him and now Pete wanted to be on his back himself.

I believe I understand now why certain jockeys suit certain racehorses. There must be some sort of affinity between man and beast. Whatever this mysterious affinity is, I certainly had it with Tournasol. He gave his all for me.

8 | A Night with a Sultan

EARLY IN THE 1930s, as chairman of the board of Pan
American Airways, I made the first passenger flight
across the mid-Pacific to China, for which I received
the Order of Blue Jade, then that country's highest
decoration. In the late 1930s when Pan Am decided to
conquer the vastness of the South Pacific islands, I was
on this pioneer flight too, escorting a group of newsmen
and dignitaries in a giant seaplane called the China
Clipper, bound for New Zealand, Australia, Bali, Java,
Borneo and the Philippines. And it promised to be a
long trip. Today's airplanes travel at five or six hundred
miles an hour at altitudes up to 40,000 feet; back in
those days they flew one hundred and fifty miles an
hour and at maximum altitude of 10,000 feet. Furthermore, en route I was to negotiate contracts with the
various countries so that Pan Am could establish regular service in the future. (World War II had already
started, but was still confined to Europe. The United
States, Japan, and China were not yet involved.) So
everything was brisk and businesslike as we hopped
the South Pacific; that is, until we came to the remote
island of Java and met a young fellow who, as far as I
knew, was the last remaining autocratic ruler in the
Far East.

A Javanese guide assigned to us by the Dutch
governor of the island met the China Clipper and escorted Eddie MacDonnel, one of the founding directors

of Pan Am, and me to the interior village of Joc Jakarta, which was ruled over by this young sultan who held every power over his twenty million subjects, including life and death. Learning of our visit, the sultan had invited Eddie and me to spend the night in his palace, the first Americans ever to be so honored.

Naturally Eddie and I were fascinated at the prospect of meeting the sultan and we plied our guide with countless questions, all of which he answered, managing to be both discreet and reasonably frank.

It seemed that the old sultan had died recently, and his son had been recalled from Oxford University to sit on the throne. By custom, the guide said, the young sultan had inherited—besides his father's kingdom—his father's numerous wives and concubines, and, at least as Eddie and I envisioned it, a life-style that sounded like something out of a Hollywood film.

The sultan lived in an ancient palace in a huge compound surrounded by a twelve-foot wall; he seldom traveled outside this royal compound. So he was seen by and, in turn, saw only those some ten thousand persons who lived within the compound, as well as—and the guide made a point of this—his pure white elephant which he liked to ride each day. And what, we asked, did the sultan do in the evening to amuse himself? Every night of his life, said the guide, after dinner he sat on his throne in the pavilion, surrounded by his wives and their ladies-in-waiting and, following ancient custom, he watched the palace dancing girls perform. This was his divertissement after what sounded like a very boring dinner, since the women couldn't dine with their lord and master.

Having already been exposed to the Hollywood scene, I had a fairly vivid imagination, so the prospect of a night spent in a sultan's palace proved more than a trifle exciting.

We were met at the huge gates of the palace by a royal guard and escorted down what seemed like miles of corridors and through dozens of great ornate doors to our magnificent quarters. As he bowed his way out of our suite of rooms, the royal guard respectfully instructed Eddie and me to be ready to meet the sultan promptly at 8:00 P.M.

Eddie and I were wondering what lay ahead for us when, promptly at eight, two menservants arrived and led us through a maze of rooms and corridors until we came to a fairly small private dining room, where dinner was set for three on a low table surrounded by squat Oriental stools. Nothing very grandiose, I thought, but entertainment will come after dinner.

Presently, our host made his entrance followed by a small entourage, one of whom disengaged himself to introduce us. Again we were surprised. The young ruler, clean-shaven, perhaps twenty-one or -two, was dressed in a tailor-made white dinner suit and white tennis shoes. He had very little of the Oriental flair we had anticipated. He proceeded to welcome us in an impeccable Oxford accent, while his servants served us Scotch and soda—very British indeed. The sultan was extremely curious about our pioneer flight and seemed most knowledgeable about all the islands of the Pacific.

Finally we sat down to dinner, a long meal with many exotic dishes and glass after glass of Japanese wines. The sultan was immensely curious about the

United States, too. He asked many questions about life there, and they were very intelligent questions too. But about his own kingdom he talked very little.

Over what may have been our third round of wine, our host sighed heavily and confessed, "I am bored to death here after my English life. All I can do is ride my elephant around and visit the wives I did not select." He looked from me to Eddie, and back again. Then he heaved another sigh, took another sip of wine and continued. "And the evenings. My God! I have to watch every night nothing except our native dancing girls. Ah, but tonight it will be different, Mr. Whitney." Different? How different? What exotic entertainment, I wondered, did the sultan have in mind? Perhaps for this pair of worldly Americans, he had concocted something really extraordinary. The way he was looking at me now, smiling, slowly nodding his head as though he could read my thoughts, I couldn't imagine what it might be. After all, a young sultan . . . an absolute ruler . . . admittedly bored. . . .

He snapped his fingers imperiously and servants instantly appeared, lining both sides of the small room. The sultan rose, folding his hands behind his back. "I am told that Americans love to play ping-pong," he said. Though it was a statement rather than a question, he paused as if waiting for a reply, and Eddie and I both rushed in to fill the silence and assure him that yes, he was absolutely correct. Americans do love to play ping-pong. The sultan smiled. "Good," he said. "I have a new English table and you fine gentlemen will play with me. I believe I can show you a trick or two," he said. "Of course you play."

"Oh yes," I said, "we play."

And so we followed the sultan out of the dining room back down the maze of rooms and corridors to a game room where we proceeded to play ping-pong. In fact, we played and played ping-pong, while from outside the window some of the most sensuous music imaginable was wafted into the room. More than a little distracting to the game. But promising.

I thought to myself: it won't be too long now before we go outside and join the fun. Ping-pong, I told myself, was simply a preliminary to more sophisticated entertainment. But the young sultan was a dedicated and apparently tireless player. A game was no sooner over than another one would begin.

Then, quite abruptly, we stopped playing. The sultan graciously bade us good night and with a clap of his hands summoned his servants. They were directed to escort us back to our quarters. "I have arranged a conducted tour of the palace compound for you at ten o'clock in the morning," he said, as we prepared to follow the servants. "And now, good night, my American friends." He reached out and enthusiastically shook our hands. "You have given me a top-hole evening. Good show."

"Good night, Your Highness," we murmured somewhat less enthusiastically, after which Eddie and I proceeded to walk down the corridor behind the servants to our living quarters. "I guess he didn't really like us," said Eddie. "Maybe he didn't trust us," I replied, and with that we fell into our cots.

The next morning, Eddie and I and some of the dignitaries on our flight took the tour of the palace compound, among them Mayor Bohron of Los Angeles, who was dressed in a formal black suit with stiff collar and tie. When we reached the cage where the sultan's white elephant was housed, the mayor asked our guide if he could please go inside and pat the beast. "I should like to tell my political friends back home of the great honor bestowed on me here," he said, and I remember wondering at the time if he was a Republican, for while I am a great animal lover myself, I couldn't understand anyone wanting to get into the cage with this huge elephant.

The guide was delighted to oblige, however. "I will open the door of the cage myself," he said, thereby upstaging the pair of uniformed men in charge of the cage.

The mayor walked with immense dignity toward the beast who, at the sight of the approaching figure, reached to the ground with its great trunk, scooped up a trunkful of manure and, taking deadly aim, hurled it smack in His Honor's face. In seconds the gentleman's entire body was stained with dripping manure. His mouth opened wide and he let out a yell of such anger that the two uniformed guards grabbed their guns. They then promptly picked up two buckets of water and doused him from head to foot.

Then, to our utter amazement, Mayor Bohron roared with laughter. From that moment till we all returned to Los Angeles he joined the group, so to speak, and we all got on famously together.

The elephant partly repaid us for the games of ping-pong.

9 | Spearhead of the Eighth Army

How, in the dramatic year 1942, did a lieutenant colonel in the U.S. Army Air Force (me), crouched down among some rocks on the desert of North Africa eating some vegetable stew, come to meet there none other than the commander-in-chief of the Eighth Army (the fabled General "Monty" Montgomery)? And wind up with an invitation to tea? But in wartime, I had already discovered, the least expected does occur.

You see, the day after the Japanese attack on Pearl Harbor in December, 1941, I, a World War I veteran, enlisted in the army air force. I was told that my calendar age (over forty) barred me from serving as an active pilot. So, undaunted, I applied for combat intelligence. After a three-months course in this branch of the service, I volunteered to go with a squadron of heavy bombers whose mission was to bomb Tokyo. I had been commissioned a major and was permitted to wear my emblem of pilot wings from World War I on my uniform. This gave me a good standing with the unit, all of whom, like me, had volunteered for this mission.

I was the waist gunner in a B-17 flying fortress when we finally got to Karachi, India. It wasn't, shall we say, on our itinerary. We were grounded there because the Japanese had taken the airport in China on which we would have landed to refuel before setting out to bomb Tokyo. After three months in India, orders came from Washington to depart with all available fighting aircraft for Cairo. General Rommel, the famous "Desert Fox" who commanded the Nazi armies in North Africa, was advancing on Alamein, and it was thought that the fall of Cairo was imminent. The British Eighth Army was, at that very moment, in full retreat across the desert.

We assembled one heavy bomber group of flying fortresses and another of P-51 air fighters and headed for Cairo—a newly formed Ninth Air Force. As things turned out, the enemy was stopped at Alamein, and in the long, hot summer of 1942, the British and Americans did all they could to reinforce the Eighth Army and plan for an attack on the Alamein positions in the fall.

I was assigned to Headquarters U.S. Desert Air Task Force about 25 miles east of Alamein at Burgel Arab. Cairo lay approximately 135 miles further south. Tents, battle wagons, and lorries covered with heavy camouflage netting were parked in properly dispersed positions. This entire encampment was mobile and could move on four hours' notice.

On October 23, the air bombardment of Alamein started, and on November 6 the German and Italian armies were routed, the Alamein line broken, and the enemy in full retreat. That evening, the entire sky was suddenly lit up as we heard the drone of German motors. And we realized we were in for some bombing. Presently, the bombs were falling all around us and I watched the fireworks from the water-filled bottom of a slit trench, fully expecting the next load to come booming down upon us. But after some twenty minutes, and still in one piece, I heard the Germans heading off across the sea toward Crete.

Our orders were to be up and standing by at five the next morning. Before daylight there was a meeting in General Montgomery's tent which General Strickland attended, and it was agreed at that time that our headquarters would break and move on to Mersa Matruh, which was expected to be clear of the enemy by the time we arrived. Actually, no one knew where our advanced units were, or exactly where the enemy was either. But everyone was anxious to get moving and to trust to luck. We were instructed to keep on the lookout for the 35 sign—a secret symbol indicating where the officers' headquarters would be for the night.

As luck would have it, heavy rains had turned the sand to mud, and the sky to the west was black and threatening. It was dangerous to risk leaving the macadam of the road and sticking in the mud, so for the first few hours we proceeded in column at about fifteen to twenty miles per hour. Everywhere we saw the litter hastily abandoned by the enemy: tanks, artillery, lorries full of stores, field kitchens, jerry cans by the hundreds, and stacks of ammunition. The further we traveled, the more evident the extent of our victory at Alamein became. Every quarter of a mile we could see where our fighter-bombers had blasted their way.

At one point we pulled off the road to where an enormous Italian supply truck stood. Soldiers were looting it, and I reached in, collected a brand new rifle and shot it, using jerry cans for targets. Then we took to the road again, in time to be all but washed away by the torrential rain that proceeded to flood us. In no time at all, the desert became a gigantic lake with little tufts of bushes sticking up through the water; rain so heavy that we could see only fifty yards to right or left. I figured that it was about here that the B-25 raid I was on three days earlier had dropped its eggs, and as we moved at a snail's pace past a group of five military transports, charred, twisted and totally wrecked, I fancied that one of the bombs I dropped had been responsible.

We came to the Fuka escarpment. The plateau there was heavily fortified with mine fields stretching to the north and south, trenches and barbed wire fences criss-crossing the entire area, and a lot of guns left in their emplacements but with their barrels blown so that we couldn't use them.

As we dropped off the plateau and headed towards the Hanneish fields, we were well over our axles in sloshing water. Even the Hanneish landing fields our fighters were supposed to occupy that day were under water. Bad luck!

Most of the vehicles on the road with us now seemed to be tanks of the Second New Zealand Division and the Eighth Heavy Armored Division. I thought it odd we were among those lads; they were supposed to be the spearhead of the Eighth Army. I concluded that they were stragglers who'd been caught in the sand by the rain and were now hurrying to catch up with their units. About ten miles farther on, we came upon 150 Italian prisoners standing by the roadside, flanked on both sides by still burning lorries.

The road improved and we picked up speed, rolling along now at forty miles an hour. According to our mileage indicator, we had come eighty-two miles. If that was correct, we were only about ten miles from

Mersa Matruh, our destination. But then as we approached the summit of a hill and saw the symbolic and very welcome 35 sign on the right, an M.P. told us we could go no further. The Nazis were shelling the ridge.

I walked up to the summit and over to one of the tanks. "Could you tell me what unit you are?" I said to a grim-looking, suntanned face. "And wouldn't you like to know!" came the reply. No rapport there, and I retreated as quickly as possible to the 35 sign where trucks and a staff car had pulled up.

"Would you like some tea?" a British army colonel asked me. I replied that I most certainly would, adding that I'd produce some of our C rations provided he'd share them. And soon the tea was boiling and the colonel and I, crouched down among the rocks, were sharing some good American meat and vegetable stew, along with sweet biscuits and chocolate bars.

What a satisfying meal that was! What utter contentment I felt! Then, suddenly, a sleek-looking staff car, flanked by two enormous Crusader tanks, pulled up to us. I looked inside the car and recognized General Montgomery himself, commanding general of the Eighth Army, sitting in the rear seat.

The British colonel and I sprang to our feet, dropping chocolate bars and sweet biscuits into the sand. I saluted—smartly, I hoped—and said, "Colonel Whitney, American air force, sir."

The general, lean and fit and bronzed by the sun, a beret jauntily tipped over his keen eyes, regarded us with no sign of anything resembling disapproval. He inquired about the tanks on the ridge ahead, but neither the colonel nor I could give a satisfactory reply. So he dispatched one of his escort tanks for the information.

In several moments the tank returned, and a smart-looking captain popped up from the manhole, saluted, and said, "It seems, General, you are the spearhead of the Eighth Army. There is a strong German position ahead, and we will have to clear it out before we can advance."

General "Monty" didn't appear fazed by that bit of military intelligence, either. He simply turned to the colonel and me and invited us to follow him for a bit of tea in a hastily erected tent where, settling down in a camp chair, he proved to be very talkative. And concerned, too, because he said accurate reports on the fighting were not coming in. The rains, he said, pausing to sip tea, were playing hell with communications. When his staff started to arrive, I quietly bowed out as he began to issue crisp, sharp orders.

And so ended the historic day after the defeat of General Rommel's army at Alamein, the turning point of World War II. And Lieutenant Colonel Whitney, U.S. Desert Air Task Force, together with General "Monty" Montgomery, commander-in-chief of the Allied forces, had actually been the spearheads of the victorious Eighth Army and were alive to tell the tale.

10 | Serpent of the Nile

I wouldn't blame anyone who reads this story for calling me a liar, but wars have their lighter sides, and truth can be stranger than fiction. So let me transport you to Cairo, Egypt, in the winter of 1942–43, at a time when World War II was in a critical stage.

I was a lieutenant colonel in the U.S. Army Air Force and had just completed two months' service at the front lines. Our air force units were attached to the British Eighth Army. From Alamein to Benghazi, our small American Desert Air Task Force had done its share in routing the enemy under the command of the Desert Fox, General Rommel. As combat intelligence officer for our air fighters, I had endured the long trek across the North African deserts and miraculously come out alive. I guess I looked pretty grubby, however, for when General Brereton flew down to Benghazi to inspect our headquarters, I weighed 138 pounds (my norm is 170), and he ordered me back to Cairo immediately for a rest. In fact, he told me to pack up and leave with him on his inspection tour of front-line air bases. So then, after a long day, the airport at Cairo looked like heaven to me.

Leaving the general at air force headquarters, I was driven to our flat in Zamalic on the island of Gezeriah, after being ordered to report for duty in ten days' time. Gezeriah at that time was a popular island in the middle of the river Nile. It contained apartments, homes, a country club, and a race course with club-house and grandstands. My chief delight there in the past summer had been playing tennis with the many excellent players from England, Australia, and South Africa.

My roommates who shared our flat, Air Commander Whitney Straight and Captain Simon Elwis, were not there when I arrived. However, our faithful servant, Mohammed, greeted me, cooked me a little supper, and so to bed without even undressing.

It did take me the ten days to repair my fatigue. In the stress of front-line duty, one somehow endures the aches and pains and worries, and relapse does not come until later.

On the fourth day, both Whitney and Simon arrived at the flat, and so we took up the congenial friendship which had existed in the summer before Alamein. And now a word about my two colorful roommates.

Air Commander Whitney Straight was my first cousin, being a son of my father's sister, Dorothy, and he was raised on the estate adjoining ours in Old Westbury, Long Island, New York. When Mr. Straight died, his mother married an Englishman, and they moved to England. Whitney became a fighter pilot when World War II hit, and he was shot down over southern France in 1941 and reported missing. He suddenly appeared in Cairo in the summer of 1942, having escaped through Spain, and we took a little flat together during the intensive days of preparation and training for the crucial battle at El Alamein.

The famous English portrait painter, Simon Elwis, whom I had known in the States, had arrived from the desert one day, and we had invited him to share our flat.

Simon, now a captain in the British army, had served a tour at the front and was assigned to British headquarters in Cairo. That arrangement led directly to the James Bond-like story which follows.

King Farouk, the handsome, young, and active ruler of Egypt favored the German rather than the Allied cause. His beautiful young Queen Fareda was stashed away in his harem and not permitted to be seen by Christian eyes, but her beauty was legendary throughout the Moslem world.

The British high command wished desperately to convert King Farouk to the British-American cause, and they came up with a plan. They commissioned our roommate, Captain Simon Elwis, to paint the portrait of the queen. Simon was not only a brilliant portrait painter, but was a young man of great personal charm. During the course of painting, he was given the mission of converting the king. Farouk wore a long, curling moustache in the German style, and Simon's first job was to get this clipped in British army style. If this was accomplished, Simon felt the rest would come easily.

King Farouk acquiesced to the portrait being painted in the queen's quarters of the harem, and, I need hardly tell you, Simon was elated. To come from tents and slit trenches on the desert to a queen's harem was more like a dream than a reality.

So, in the following days, while Whitney and I were slaving at headquarters with problems of war, Simon Elwis was slaving in his fashion in the harem of Her Majesty, Queen Fareda of Egypt. In the evenings, Simon kept us entertained with accounts of his doings, and progress on the portrait.

He was painting her sitting on her throne with a crown on her head and dressed in regal robes. He told us that her beauty and charm exceeded his wildest imagination. He felt his mission of converting the king was proceeding according to plan, but not as yet accomplished. The German moustache was being trimmed, but Farouk still disliked England and the United States. He must prolong his stay, so he had persuaded the queen to let him paint her in her riding habit, and then, he hoped, as a nymph in her garden. I guess he fancied himself to be a reincarnation of Romney, the great English painter, who had followed the same formula with the English beauty, Lady Hamilton.

One evening, Simon informed us that he had told the queen about Whitney and me, our youth together in the United States, and our reunion in the air force in Egypt. She was craving to meet both of us, and they had devised a plan of how it could be done. We listened with bated breath. The great Egyptian prince, Mohammed Ali, would be giving a party in his fabulous palace next Saturday night, to which Whitney and I would be invited. On the stroke of midnight an Egyptian man would tap me on the shoulder, and I would follow him to her private quarters. About one-half hour later the man would reappear and lead me back to the grand ballroom. He would then do the same procedure with Air Commander Whitney Straight.

"And what if we are caught?" I asked.

"It is true, Sonny," replied Simon, "that the king keeps a close watch on her, but this will be very carefully planned, and the man who will guide you is her most trusted servant."

And so the talk went on among the three of us

and, you can guess it, we could not resist the adventure, no matter how risky it might be.

Saturday night finally came, and Whitney and I were dolled up in our best-fitting dress uniforms. It was one of those full moon nights in winter that only Cairo can put on.

The party was magnificent beyond all attempts to describe, some two hundred guests, the ladies adorned with priceless jewels. The Pashas were in Oriental garb, and the military of many nations were in full dress with decorations. Dinner was served in seven courses on golden plates with an attendant in colorful uniform behind each gilt-encrusted chair. Music from a hidden orchestra played tunes from the various countries represented.

After dinner the men and women separated, and we guys were served coffee and liqueurs by beautiful harem girls as we squatted on individual hassocks. For our entertainment a few belly dancers performed to soft Oriental rhythms. Then the grand ball started, and the ballroom filled with people. Having been stationed in Cairo for some six months the previous year, I knew most of the people present, so I was able to find many dancing partners.

The ballroom was two stories high, and along one wall on the upper level was an intricate Arab latticework paneling. I knew that behind this was the queen's private chamber where she could see the goings-on but not be seen herself. I glanced at my watch. It read three minutes until zero hour. I took my stand close to a doorway where I was less conspicuous, for I wore the only American uniform present.

Suddenly I received a tap on the shoulder, and I turned to follow a small man dressed in Egyptian uniform. Not a word was spoken as we wove our way through corridors, up and down stairways, and finally came to a halt before a great bronze door. He slid the bolt and made a deep bow for me to enter.

The young queen sat on an improvised settee surrounded by her handmaidens who were gently fanning her with ostrich-feather fans. Simon had not exaggerated her fatal beauty, and her face radiated her personality and intelligence. Music from the ballroom below filled the incense-laden air. I made a formal bow and kissed the extended delicate hand. She motioned me to sit down and said in clear-cut English, "Colonel Whitney, your good friend Simon Elwis has told me much about you. I asked him to arrange this meeting, for I do not know any Americans, and I want to know them and learn more about your country. I love your jazz music, and a friend sends me records. Will you have some champagne with me?"

And so started a fabulous half hour. She set me completely at ease. I was surprised how well informed she was on current world events and the progress of the great war.

I could not resist asking her to dance with me, and she happily accepted. So, in this romantic setting we danced a waltz and a fox trot, drank champagne, and nibbled on assorted pastries. There was then a loud knock on the door, and my unwelcome guide appeared. I kissed her hand goodbye, gave her beautiful harem girls an American army salute, and disappeared into the pitch black corridor outside. I drove back to our little flat in Zamalic and decided to stay up until cousin Whitney arrived so that we could compare notes. It was actually not too long before he barged into the room in obvious excitement.

"My God, Sonny, I hope you fared better than I. Farouk's bodyguard caught me and threw me out, screaming that he would report me to the king. What do you think I should do?"

So we discussed the situation back and forth, and in the end, decided to await further developments before reporting the disaster to our commanding generals. And it is this subsequent event which climaxes this Egyptian fairy tale. It occurred some ten days later when one evening Simon, Whitney, and I were sitting around the fire in our flat drinking an after-dinner Kommermeyer tea.

There was a loud pounding on our door at about the hour of midnight. I strode to the door and gingerly started to open it, when a strong arm appeared and forced it open, pushing me backward. A short, stocky Egyptian with two huge revolvers strapped to his waist entered the room followed by another man dressed in British army shorts and bush jacket. His face was covered with scraggly hair and a short scraggly beard— obviously a disguise. All three of us knew at once that it was the great King Farouk, for it was well known that he traveled around Cairo at night in disguise.

"Please come in," I said, having no alternative.

He strode over to me, shook his finger in my face, and said, "Colonel Whitney, I have no use for your country or your secretary of state, Mr. Cordell Hull. One year ago, he promised me fourteen automobiles, and I have received none."

Then, turning to Whitney Straight, he shouted,

"And England, too, does not keep her promises. I made a mechanical invention, and I was promised the royalties from it. Have I received any? No. Your country, Air Commander Straight, cannot be trusted. Have you anything to say?"

"No, Your Majesty," replied Whitney. "There must be an explanation."

The king then strode over to Simon and said, "Captain Elwis, may I look through your apartment? Yes. Then please show me the way."

When they were gone, Whitney called Mohammed and ordered him to bring coffee and brandy. The bodyguard stood squarely blocking the exit door with both hands on his guns.

In about fifteen minutes, Simon and the king returned, and the latter plumped himself down in a chair and looked from one to the other of us. Then, for the next two hours we sat thus, sipping coffee and brandy, and carrying on a stilted conversation about the war and politics.

We thought our uninvited visitor and his evil-looking bodyguard would never leave. Then suddenly he rose, and we all did likewise, strode over next to Simon, and said with a suave smile, "Captain Elwis, I do not think you are familiar with our eastern customs. I shall enlighten you. When a man displeases us, his body is found floating in our Mother River, the Nile, with his throat slit open, and the serpent of the Nile is happily devouring him. And now, gentlemen, I thank you for your hospitality and bid you a goodbye and a good night's rest." So saying, he shook each of us by the hand, strode to the door and vanished into the night with his bodyguard beside him.

"My God," cried Simon, "he looked in every closet and under every bed in the flat. What do you think he expected to find?"

"It is quite obvious, Simon," said Whitney with a grin. "Did you steal anything from the harem, old boy?"

"Oh, no, really," stammered Simon, "I was trying so hard to convert him to our side. Do you think, fellows, I might have overdone it, overstayed my welcome?"

"Yes, I think you did exactly that. You've made him jealous. So, what shall we do now?" said I.

"I know what I will do," said Whitney. "I shall report the whole affair to my commander first thing in the morning."

Simon and I agreed to do the same, and so on and on, and then to bed.

Whitney and I received sympathetic hearings and so remained at our posts, but our talented friend, Captain Simon Elwis, was dispatched the next day on a secret mission to the Island of Madagascar, if memory serves me correctly.

11 | Yankee Maid at Iwo Jima

IN MARCH, 1943, I was recalled from Africa to serve at headquarters in the Pentagon, where I was assigned to the Plans Division under General Kuter. In February, 1945, the American forces were closing in on Japan and the major assault was imminent. If successful, it was hoped that this would trigger the surrender of Japan and the end of World War II.

Jim Forrestal, our secretary of the navy and a personal friend, requested that I be appointed Army Air Force adviser to him and accompany him on the forthcoming invasion. The request was granted, and we departed on the secretary's DC-4 the evening of February 10. At Saipan, we boarded Task Force 55 of the fleet and embarked with the assault forces for Iwo Jima. Nine days later, on D-Day, from our position on the command ship S.S. *El Dorado* anchored about one mile off the landing beaches, we could see the whole beach area in a mass of flames and smoke. So, once again, I was an eyewitness to history in the making.

The battle on shore continued to rage for three more days. On the fourth day, when it appeared that our forces would finally rout the Japanese, Mr. Forrestal invited me to accompany him on a trip along the shoreline of Iwo and, if conditions were satisfactory, to land on Red Beach.

We moved across an extremely rough sea toward Suribachi, a forbidding-looking place with its shattered crags, boulders, and volcanic ash. Such vegetation as it once had had been burned off by exploding shells. That human beings had been able to live and fight on this mass of rock was nothing short of amazing, and now—this very morning—the marines were going to scale it, while some several hundred of the enemy were preparing to defend it to the last man.

The Japanese had shelled Red Beach early that morning, and it was felt that there was some time yet to spare before they would start shelling it again, so it was decided that we could go ashore. We piled aboard an LSVP, a rectangular craft looking something like a huge bathtub, and, crouching low to avoid being hit by shrapnel, our craft leapt toward the beach at a speed of about twenty miles an hour. Instructions were to prepare for the shock as we hit the beach and, the moment the forward door opened, to run as fast as possible and make for the first trench. Needless to say, we followed those instructions to the letter.

While we were getting back our breath, General Holland Smith, who was acting as our guide, lowered his field glasses and, pointing toward Mount Suribachi, said, "Look up there. The marines are near the top."

I can tell you it was a thrilling sight. Our men were scrambling up the almost perpendicular walls, appearing to be only a few yards from the summit. I could see smoke puffs from their rifles and some marines hurling hand grenades, when suddenly five or six men appeared silhouetted against the sky. It was plain that they were marines. We all watched them walking to the left at what appeared to be almost a snail's pace, stopping occasionally to fire or duck behind boulders.

Then it appeared! Against the clear blue of the

Pacific sky we saw the American flag rising. A cheer went up from the men around us. I turned to look at General Smith, and saw tears streaming down the face of this seasoned veteran. "I told you they'd do it," he said.

I had never seen our flag raised before upon a battlefield, and I probably never shall see it again. I can only tell you that it was an unforgettable sight.

A few hundred yards inland we stopped around a typical Jap dugout where, in the soft, blood-stained sands, marines swarmed around us. That very morning the last two Japanese in the dugout had been killed and, just beyond, a stack of some one hundred Japanese bodies scented the morning air. A marine standing close to the secretary told him that the night before a man had arisen from this pile of dead bodies and taken a shot at him.

Meantime, gunfire from the battle area seemed to be increasing, and a large battery, concealed underground near us, began to return fire. General Smith appeared to be getting extremely nervous; having responsibility for the safety of the secretary of the navy wasn't to his liking. "I wish I hadn't done this," he whispered to me, "but the secretary insisted on coming ashore. What was I to do?" Evidently he made up his mind to do something decisive, for only minutes later, he muttered to me, "Well, I'm going to get him out of here now!" Addressing himself to the secretary, he said, "Sir, I wish to report that Red Beach is under shell fire, and I urge you to leave at once."

Following the general's lead, we made a dash for the LSVP and in a few moments were out beyond reach of the shells already falling upon the beach.

About four hundred yards out, we scrambled aboard the gunboat whose captain, a smart-looking young navy lieutenant, saluted the secretary and asked if he wouldn't care to have lunch. So there we were, the sounds of battle echoing in our ears, rolling and tossing a few hundred yards off the beach at Iwo, devouring fried chicken and apple pie a la mode.

Halfway through lunch, the captain informed me that the cook who had prepared our all-American feast requested permission to come up on deck and speak to me. And in a moment, a smiling black man emerged from the hold, walked up to me and said, "Aren't you the Colonel Whitney who has a farm in Lexington, Kentucky?"

"I am indeed," I replied.

Saluting smartly, he said, "Colonel, could you tell me how is old Yankee Maid?"

I looked at him in amazement. Yankee Maid was one of my best racing mares and had many foals which had been enormously successful at the tracks.

"I used to take care of her at your farm," the cook continued. "How is she? Has she got any foals at the races this year?"

"No, I regret she hasn't," I replied. And upon hearing that, the cook looked as though he regretted it as much as I did. We chatted for a few minutes more and then, with another snappy salute, this enormously cheerful fellow disappeared back into the hold. For those moments spent chatting with him, it was as though the earthy aroma of the stable blew through the acrid smell of battle. When I took my seat at the dining table, I looked across at Secretary Forrestal who, having overheard this conversation between a pair of horse racing fans, was grinning, momentarily distracted and looking relaxed for the first time since we had left Washington. We all finished our apple pie a la mode in an almost festive mood. Our flag now fluttered over Mount Suribachi, and the cook and the apple pie were most welcome reminders of home.

Later we returned to the *El Dorado*, packed our equipment and were transferred to a destroyer. At five o'clock in the afternoon we put to sea in the direction of Guam. It was a clear and cloudless afternoon. My last memory of Iwo is of another air raid alarm. On the radar screen we could see about twenty-five Japanese airplanes approaching the island, and, as we went along at a thirty-five-mile clip, we could faintly hear the roar of the fleet's guns greeting them.

In addition to the raising of the American flag on a battle-scarred hill at Iwo, I recall, with emotion, a wounded marine telling me that the biggest moment of the war for him was shaking hands with the secretary of the navy, standing there in the bloody sands beside him.

Mr. Forrestal did not do this to impress. He did it through instinct, which is part of our democratic heritage. Some of us are cast in higher roles than others, and perform according to our assignments. Yet, most of us do not lose the common touch. The navy had, in its secretary, a typical American, human and humorous, who wished to share some of the hardships of his command. The action was natural with him, as it was with the black cook who wished to pay his respects to his former boss.

12 | Taming of the Bear

ON JUNE 17, 1973, the *Herald-Leader*, our Lexington, Kentucky, newspaper, carried the following U.P.I. message from Berlin, Germany: "On the 25th anniversary of the Soviet blockade of Berlin, the city anxiously looks ahead toward the role it will play now that the Communist threat appears to be ended. During the 320-day Blockade, which began June 19, 1948, West Berlin was called 'the outpost of freedom.'"

As I read the above, I suddenly recalled the part I played in terminating that historic blockade of Berlin. The story has never been told. Here it is.

About thirty years ago, in 1948, I was assistant secretary of the air force. Early one morning in June—8:30 A.M., to be exact—I was summoned to the top secret room in the Pentagon by an urgent message from Mr. Forrestal, the secretary of defense. It was a small gathering: the secretaries of war and navy, General Vandenberg, commander of the air force, and me, for Secretary Symington, then absent from the country, had appointed me acting secretary. So once again I was, so to speak, sitting in the first row watching history in the making, and this time about to take an unexpectedly active part.

Looking not a little concerned, Secretary Forrestal got right down to business. "General Lucius Clay is on the telephone from Berlin," he said, "and I wish you gentlemen to pick up your telephones and listen." We did, and here are General Clay's words as I remember them: "Mr. Secretary, the situation in Berlin is critical. Russian air fighters are over Berlin trying to break up our air fighters escorting the cargo planes with supplies and provisions into Berlin. Both sides are getting trigger-happy, and this morning we have had some actual shooting. Two planes were hit and forced down. I don't think I can hold the situation in control any longer. I request that you dispatch immediately from the United States an air force bomber group loaded with the atomic bomb for action. The group must be here tomorrow morning, as we may be in a war. This is my unchangeable position as commander of American forces in Berlin."

We had time for only a moment of stunned silence before Mr. Forrestal was addressing us as follows: "Gentlemen, I am calling an emergency meeting of the National Security Council in the president's office at the White House at two o'clock this afternoon. I wish the secretaries of each service to be prepared to say what they can do in the event of war." Then looking pointedly at each of us, he added, "Any questions?" There were no questions, and Mr. Forrestal promptly adjourned the meeting, saying that he would see us all at two o'clock at the White House.

I returned post haste to my office and called General Larry Norstaad, asking him to rush over. He arrived pronto, and after telling him the situation, he proceeded to brief me on our capabilities.

The air force, I was told, had a heavy bomb group stationed in Newfoundland ready to take off on short notice. However—and here was the blow—although they had an atomic bomb there, it would take too long to arm it in order to reach Berlin by the next morning. I told him to see that the group was alerted for possible takeoff any time after 3:00 P.M. that day.

I then busied myself finding out what the capabilities of the U.S. Air Force were in the event of war with the Russians: number of fighting units, their whereabouts and state of readiness. Next, I contacted combat intelligence to acquire their information regarding Soviet air capabilities. Meantime, I was facing the two o'clock deadline with no decisive course of action in mind. But then I learned, through another source, that there was a man in Washington who had entree to the Russian embassy there, a man whom the Soviets trusted. I ordered him sent to me at once. I decided I would take him with me to the White House, but have him remain outside in the official car with my driver. I had a plan—fraught with danger, no question of that—but in my book, the only one which might succeed. I had been awarded the Distinguished Service Medal for having made some critical combat decisions in World War II, and now I felt the urge to risk another.

At a quarter of two o'clock, members of the National Security Council were arriving in the oval room at the White House and taking their protocol seats at the immense mahogany table. Promptly at two o'clock the president entered, took his seat and asked Secretary of State George Marshall to call the meeting to order.

Harry Truman looked his usual decisive self, neatly dressed in a grey business suit and with a pleasant smile on his face. I had known him now, both in and out of office hours, quite intimately for more than a year.

It was a pleasure working for him because he made up his mind promptly. He never kept you dangling with indecision.

The secretaries of the three armed services were promptly called on in order of their seniority: army, navy, and last but not least, air force.

The army had a number of engineer battalions guarding the access bridges to Berlin. These could be relied upon to keep the bridges open in minor incidents, but not in the event of open war with the Soviets.

The navy, as I recall it, had one marine division in Panama, and one on the island of Guam in the Pacific. It would take considerable time to transport them by ship and air to Germany.

And now, what could the youngest service, the U.S. Air Force, do?

It was my moment on stage center, and knowing the president's passion for straight talk, I wasted no time getting to the point. "Mr. President," I said, "we have a long-range bombing group stationed in New-foundland and I have given them orders to stand by for dispatch to Berlin. The atomic bomb is armed and has been put aboard. The group can take off at eight o'clock tonight, which should put them in the critical area by ten o'clock tomorrow morning. It is my considered recommendation that this course of action be adopted."

A half hour of spirited discussion followed, after which the president called for a vote. My recommendation was adopted and the meeting dismissed. I walked rapidly over to President Truman, who was about to leave, and said in his ear, "It's urgent, sir, that I see you immediately in your office." He didn't appear surprised. "Certainly, Whitney," he said. "Come along."

When we were alone in his private office I made my confession. "Mr. President," I said, "I lied to the Security Council. The group is alerted and ready to go as I said, but we cannot arm the bomb in time. However, Mr. President, I have a man waiting outside in my car who will advise the Russian embassy here in Washington that the group has been dispatched with the bomb armed and with orders to use it."

I don't know what I had expected, but I must say that what happened surprised me. Mr. Truman leaped from his chair, grabbed me by the hand and shook it with great strength, saying, "Good work, Whitney. I approve your actions. You may proceed with the plan."

The president then dismissed me and I returned to my waiting car to give the proper orders to my man regarding his mission at the Russian embassy. But there remained one more very important detail. Secretary of Defense Forrestal had to give the order to General Vandenberg to dispatch the bomb group.

At my office there was a message for me from Mr. Forrestal asking me to meet him at his residence in Georgetown at six o'clock. I called General Vandenberg and asked him to stand by the telephone from six on, for the order. Then, for me, it was back home for a brief rest, then on to the secretary's house.

It was a pleasantly warm evening and we enjoyed an excellent dinner. Conversation, not surprisingly, revolved around the dramatic events of the day, and our talk reminded me of the hours I spent with Jim Forrestal during the war. I was becoming increasingly edgy, however, as the fateful hour of eight o'clock approached. I looked at my watch and finally said, "Mr. Secretary, General Vandenberg is standing by for your command to proceed with the mission." I rose and handed him the telephone which rested on a nearby table. He dialed, gave the order, and then put the phone back in its cradle. He looked at me for a moment, and then he said cheerfully, "Let's have a nightcap and try to get a good night's sleep." And so home I went soon afterward and, surprisingly, I did have a good night's sleep.

At eight the next morning, I was at my desk and on the alert. When the phone rang, I lunged for it, picking it up on the first ring. It was Jim Forrestal, and the timbre of his voice told me automatically that he had good news. And how right I was!

"General Lucius Clay just phoned to say that he had been advised by the Russian command that the blockade of Berlin has been ordered terminated." He paused for only the briefest moment and then continued, "General Clay has issued orders to ground the U.S. air fighters, and now peace and quiet reigns in Berlin. Mission successfully completed." With that, he hung up.

And I mopped my brow and promptly ordered a cup of black coffee.

13 | How Come Kentucky?

I HAVE been asked a thousand times what made me finally decide to spend so much time on my farm in Kentucky when I used to visit it for a maximum of about ten days a year. The answer to this is interesting and dramatic.

I was riding high in the year 1958, because in January I had married the girl of my dreams, Marie Louise Hosford. She is better known today as Marylou, and to me, for some unknown reason, as Mary.

We had both suffered from unhappy marriages when we met in Scottsdale, Arizona. I was producing movies then and I had her starred opposite Lee Marvin and Gary Merrill in a picture called *Missouri Traveler*. She came from the prominent Schroeder family in Kansas City, so the casting seemed appropriate.

She was blonde, petite, and very feminine, yet outgoing, outspoken, and efficient; we fell in love during the making of the picture. She had four children whom she cherished with love and discipline. I, too, learned to love M'lou, Heather, Hobbs, and Hank. Mary and I started enjoying life and people again and were even eager to accept the challenges of marriage. She is a Capricorn and I am a Pisces, so I had to understand her practicality and she had to learn about a dreamer who strove to bring his dreams to reality.

Mary had majored in dramatic arts and I had been brought up in an artistic setting with my mother, the sculptress Gertrude Vanderbilt Whitney. So we had this in common and also a love of everything to do with the outdoor life, she through her father, Harry Schroeder, and I through my father, the outdoor sportsman Harry Payne Whitney.

So in January, 1958, we were married in Reno, Nevada, and, believe it or not, I took her to Flin Flon, Manitoba, Canada, for a honeymoon. We went by train to Winnipeg, and then in the mining company's prop plane on skis to land in two feet of snow and temperatures forty below zero at Flin Flon, six hundred miles north of Winnipeg. There had been nothing but a wilderness of forest, streams, and lakes beneath us, and flying at only two thousand feet we had seen plenty of moose, bears, deer, and wolves.

I had founded and was chairman of the board of the mining company, so we lodged in Whitney House which had a 20 x 20 foot combined living and dining room, kitchen, two 8 x 10 foot bedrooms, and one bathroom with shower. There was almost no furniture. Mary decided to remedy this, and the company executives' wives told her the only place to get furniture was Winnipeg. Instead she walked up and down the only street in Flin Flon, stopped in every store and wound up furnishing the entire cottage. For this thoughtful act she became the uncrowned queen of Flin Flon.

We then returned to Beverly Hills, California, to ready ourselves for a whistle-stop tour from San Francisco to Chicago to promote her forthcoming *Missouri Traveler Cookbook*. By the time we reached Chicago I was eager to have her see my horse farm in Kentucky. So there we went.

I think she had expected a southern mansion, but

instead she saw a small red brick cottage. My farm manager and his wife, Ivor and Frances Balding, were in residence, so we squeezed into one tiny bedroom and bathroom suite.

I had recently acquired a sixty-acre addition to the farm which had on it an early pioneer house on a small hilltop overlooking Elkhorn Creek. Mary was dying to see it. So the next morning we took a picnic lunch and hiked across the frozen fields and climbed the hill to the house.

It was indeed a lovely site, but the house was in need of extensive repairs and improvements, and the grounds were in shocking condition. I was looking it over in despair when Mary exclaimed, "Sonny, this is a challenge. I know you only spend about ten days a year on this farm, but I'd like to renovate and improve the whole layout. It's a very old and probably historic house, maybe you could rent it. I'll tell you what. If you will fix up the grounds which is your thing, I will renovate the house. It's a project."

So we wandered about and looked and looked, and I agreed with her. Back to the cottage, we talked it all over with Ivor and Frances. Decisions were made and soon Mary and I were on the way back to California. We had decided to return in early May to see the Kentucky Derby.

What a different Kentucky it was when we returned to the little brick cottage on my farm, the trees and fields all green, and the mares and foals and yearlings grazing and running and playing in every pasture. Ivor and Frances Balding greeted us warmly and soon we were sipping delicious mint juleps.

We learned that my cousin Joan Payson, who was

next door on Greentree Farm, had invited us to a pre-Derby cocktail and dinner party, and that all the prominent horse people would be there. So of course we accepted. I had met very few local people on my previous visits to the farm, as Ivor Balding was a dirt farmer. He lived on the farm and for the farm and the livestock. He rarely, if ever, attended social functions. His ambition was to produce good horses through good farm practices, so daily he walked the pastures and studied all the up-to-date theories on nutrition.

Mary and I decided to get to the party early so that we could mingle with the Kentucky people. The Greentree house was indeed a southern mansion with pillars and everything, and we were greeted with open arms by cousin Joan and Charlie Payson. Then people started to arrive and we had our first taste of warm southern hospitality. Pre-Derby fever and excitement filled the air with chatter and laughter. In sharp contrast to Hollywood lovelies with their brightly colored dresses, the Kentucky belles wore very prim and proper outfits. Even that could not hide their beauty and charm which was very appealing to male eyes. The men, if I can recall correctly, wore neatly fitting business suits with matching ties and shirts.

When dinner finally was announced we were shown to our seats at tables of eight, which were scattered in various rooms. Mary and I were not only at different tables, but in different rooms.

Dinner was almost over and coffee about to be served, when Mary came running to my table and in a breathless voice, half whispered to me, "Take me to Mrs. Duval Headley right away, quick, do you know where she is?"

"No, I don't," said I, "but I know her and we'll find her." Her husband Duval Headley, nephew of the well known horseman Hal Price Headley, had been head of the Greentree Farm operations, and I did know him and his charming wife Betty from my previous visits.

"I've done something awful," said Mary hysterically to me as we pushed our way through the rooms in search of Betty. Then suddenly I saw her seated on the stairway with an admiring group around her and I rushed Mary up and introduced her.

"I must tell you what I've done. I didn't mean to," stammered Mary. "I got your husband into a duel." Betty looked up inquiringly. "It happened this way," continued Mary. "Mr. de Roulet told my whole table in a loud voice that no man should marry a girl unless he could afford a cook. That it was not proper to expect a lady to cook for her husband. After those words your husband, who was seated on my right, rose to his feet and said to de Roulet, 'You, sir, have insulted Miss Mary, my wife, Betty, and all the good people at this table. They have all been brought up to cook and keep house. Miss Mary as you well know is not only a fine cook, but has written a cookbook. I demand satisfaction on the dueling grounds tomorrow morning and you, sir, can choose the weapons.'"

I admit that when Mary finished I was as surprised and confused as she. There was a moment of charged silence and then Betty reached for Mary's hand and looking up into her eyes calmly said, "Think nothing of it, honey, my Duval is a real good shot." She then turned back to her group and continued with the party chatter.

I then took Mary back to where everyone was milling around in the pre-Derby fever. We stayed for a while, then found the Baldings and decided to go home.

On the way back in the car Mary told her story to Ivor and Frances, and Ivor said, "Don't worry, Marylou, you don't know Duval. Yes, he meant what he said about cooking. You may not know it, but every girl at your table was an excellent cook and housekeeper. But the dueling bit was done to make us northerners think that this still goes on in Kentucky. And de Roulet— well, he loves to start an argument."

"Are you sure?" said Mary. "If you are, I kind of like it." And we all laughed and relaxed.

Later that night, as Mary and I were sipping a good-night julep, she leaned against me and said, "You know, I think I would like it here."

"Let's talk about it tomorrow," I murmured, and so to bed.

In conclusion may I say that on the morrow we did sit on the hilltop near our new house and decided to wind up our life in California as soon as was practical and try out Kentucky. Thus can major decisions affecting one's way of life sometimes be made when one least expects it.

14 | Buffalo Bill Cody

MY MOTHER, Gertrude Vanderbilt Whitney, got involved with Buffalo Bill when the family took a trip on our private Pullman car, "Wanderer," in the early 1920s, to see a bit of the Far West.

I knew the name Buffalo Bill because my greatest thrill as a young boy in New York City had been to go to the "Wild West Show" in Madison Square Garden. Colonel Cody, alias Buffalo Bill, Annie Oakley, real Indians, and cowboys from the plains put on such a show as we easterners had only dreamed of. I remember today one scene in the show where a real western stagecoach was attacked by the Indians, and a battle between them and the cowboys ensued. At one performance, I rode in the stagecoach. Why I was invited is still unknown to me, but what a thrill! And now I had been told that Cody, Wyoming, was on our itinerary. This would indeed be the Wild West of song and story for me.

I don't remember now where all the trip took us, but we wound up in Yellowstone Park by automobile, and then on to Cody. I recall it was there we met Buffalo Bill's niece, Mary Jester Allen. She and my mother got together and must have been very simpatico, for my mother purchased forty acres of land which she donated to the town of Cody to create a museum complex of western art. In order to start the project, she agreed to create and sculpt a lifesize statue of Buffalo Bill, who had died in 1917, and erect it on the site which she had chosen.

My mother did exactly that, and the statue was unveiled at Cody in 1927. The first building, a log cabin to house some of Colonel Cody's treasures, had been opened to the public by Mary Jester Allen, but I did not have the time to go out to see it. My mother's world and mine were completely separate, although our relationship was very close and affectionate.

Then came World War II, and I enlisted in the army air force and served in India, North Africa, the invasion of Iwo Jima in the Pacific, then at headquarters in Washington until the end of the war. My dear mother had passed away while I was in India in 1942.

After the war was over, I received a letter from Mary Jester Allen inviting me to visit Cody and attend a summer rodeo there. I accepted, went out and was housed in Buffalo Bill Cody's own Hotel Irma. I looked in awe and reverence at my mother's heroic statue. Buffalo Bill, the scout, is seated on a truly western pony, his right arm extended upward and forward, holding a rifle, his left reining in the pony, and head bent earthward staring at the earth beneath. He has seen Indian footprints in the sand, and is signalling his scouts to come quickly. The monument is in bronze, and, I am told, weighs twenty-four tons. Next to the four horsemen, who stand in front of the cathedral in Venice, Italy, it is the largest equestrian statue in the world.

I was then taken by Mary Jester Allen to a chuckwagon lunch. The settlers from the surrounding ranches were camped in their prairie wagons around a large field on the outskirts of town. I was taken from one to the other, introduced and offered various snacks of food. Some of these people were truly picturesque in their western costumes and Indian jewelry.

At one wagon a very spry old man (I was told he was over 90) asked me if I liked to hunt elk. I told him I liked to hunt, but had never hunted elk. He replied that if I had the weekend free, he would be glad to guide me in the high mountains which surround Cody. When I replied that I could not accept his kind invitation, he shook his head and said, "Young man, I am truly sorry, for you look young and healthy and strong, and I believe you could follow me over them hills. You see this wagon here? Well, I come here in it with my family across the plains before there was any railroad west of the Missouri, and I ain't through travelin' yet."

I have thought about this old man's statement many times since. We don't stop to think what a really new and young country we still were after World War II; the strongest military and industrial power, and suddenly placed in the position of having to dominate the policies of the world. It is not surprising that we have made mistakes, but it is in the American tradition to persist, and I, for one, am confident that we shall succeed.

That same afternoon we toured the forty acres my mother had given to the city upon which to create a lasting memory of Buffalo Bill, to display the white and Indian arts and the cultures of the western plains. The forty acres were still almost wild, save for her statue, which dominated the spectacular landscape.

The Irma Hotel was exactly as it had been when Buffalo Bill lived there. I don't believe Cody itself had changed much. The men still wore guns, dressed in real western style, and cow ponies were visible on the dirt streets with grinning cowboys astride them.

I was introduced to such famous local characters as Larry Larom, Ernest Gopperty, Freddy Garlow, Peggy Coe, Glenn Nielson and others. After several get-togethers, I agreed to launch the memorial center by donating the money to build a gallery of western art in memory of my mother. She had been the first person of authority to recognize and promote American artists. She had founded the Whitney Museum of American Art in New York. Certainly a museum of American art of the West would be an appropriate memorial. Cody, Wyoming, was the logical site as already standing there was her monumental equestrian statue of Buffalo Bill.

Mary Jester Allen then told me the fabulous story about my mother while she was working on the statue of Buffalo Bill. She had wanted an authentic western pony as a model, so one was sent east to Long Island with a young cowboy to take care of him. The cowboy's name happened to be Will Rogers.

One evening in New York City, Mr. Flo Ziegfeld invited my mother to attend a rehearsal of the Ziegfeld Follies, which was on the verge of its gala opening. At the end of the rehearsal, Mr. Ziegfeld was tearing his hair and ranting and raving that the show lacked a comedian. My mother told him about the statue she was creating, and that the young cowboy who was caring for the pony kept her constantly amused with his stories and dry sense of humor. She said he would stand there twisting and coiling his lariat while he talked. Ziegfeld said, "Can you get hold of him imme-diately?" She did, and he held up the rehearsal until

Will arrived. The rest is history, for Will Rogers appeared with the show on opening night and was a smashing success. In fact, despite the beautiful Ziegfeld girls, he stole the show. Will Rogers, like Bob Hope today, did not have to rely on vulgarity to hold his audiences.

The culmination and the high peak for me of this story came in the year 1959, when the Buffalo Bill Historical Center was formally dedicated. My wife Mary and I were invited, and I was asked to be the principal speaker for the occasion.

Believe it or not, we were lodged in Buffalo Bill Cody's own apartment in the Irma Hotel. It was as the colonel had left it, no closets or drawers, and we had to hang our clothes on pegs along one wall. There were three days of festivities, culminating in the dedication ceremonies in the public school's reception hall. I made my speech to a room packed with dignitaries who had travelled there from as far away as Texas and California.

Then we proceeded to the Whitney Gallery, whose exhibit halls had been completed. The director of the gallery, Edward McCracken, escorted us through.

I have been in many museums during my life, in the United States, Europe, the Middle East, and the Orient. This gallery stood up with the best, in its technique of exhibit and quality of the works displayed. From the great northern window, one looked out upon my mother's statue of Buffalo Bill with a backdrop of the snow-capped Rocky Mountains beyond.

I, as my mother always did, believed that our American artists could hold their own against any competition. I ask the reader to go to see for himself.

This day gave the necessary impetus toward the completion of the entire historical center, which is going ahead by leaps and bounds. In 1976 we dedicated a new wing donated by the Winchester Arms Company, and we are now raising the money necessary for a third wing, which will exhibit the arts and crafts of the Plains Indians.

I offer a salute to Buffalo Bill, the inspiration, and to my mother, the farsighted American artist who helped make all this possible.

15 | Whence Cometh My Help

THE OUTDOORS has played a very important part in my life. I have had many exciting adventures in the outdoors, but here I am going to narrate the kind of experience which almost anyone can have in this amazing country of ours. If you live either in a city or in its suburb, you can take advantage of the wonderful opportunities which the more remote areas offer.

Kentucky prides itself in its system of state parks, which are situated within an hour to an hour-and-a-half drive from all its centers of population. This enables the working man to take his family out of the cities on his days off and enjoy a healthy vacation in the country. Such a break from routine is a great moment for most persons. It is for me.

The bluegrass section of Kentucky is situated in the central part of the state and is surrounded east and west by the hill country. So let me tell you about one such day off on the hills. It happened last June with our eldest boy, Hobbs, my caretaker Jouett Redmon, and myself. We loaded the International Travelall with our fishing gear and took off at about eleven in the morning, our destination the Natural Bridge State Park, following the Bert Combs Mountain Parkway which winds through Appalachia and terminates at Prestonsburg some hundred miles ahead. One slowly leaves the bluegrass country behind, as rolling pasture lands with great herds of cattle fan out on both sides. Finally that, too, is replaced by Clay City at the entrance to the hill country. From there the road winds through a wide valley with mountains on both sides, and the valley slowly narrowing until one comes to the head of it at Slade. The trees on the hills are in their first brilliant greens, and the wild dogwood flowers are visible. We exit from the parkway at Slade, and the road climbs through the state park and up a steep hill to Hemlock Lodge. We have made the trip in one hour. The view from the dining room of the lodge is spectacular, with a lake directly below and the high limestone cliffs above, terminating with the majestic natural bridge of limestone rock silhouetted against the sky. We lunch on homemade bean soup, fresh perch from the creek and a delicious cherry cobbler to top it off. The atmosphere is quiet and restful. We have already left far behind the bustle of city life.

After lunch we take to the road again, back to the parkway and on through the mountains to Prestonsburg. Our destination, Jenny Wiley State Park, lies a few miles beyond, and we reach the lodge at about four in the afternoon. I had made reservations in advance, so we are shown to two attractive adjoining rooms with outdoor balconies overlooking a pine-clad hillside and Dewey Lake below. High mountains surround the lake, and the slopes are resplendent with the spring colors and blossoms.

We have come here to fish the lake and tomorrow explore the remote country to the north where I have pinpointed a mountain stream which the state stocks with rainbow trout. This park is named for Jenny Wiley, daughter of a pioneer family who, some 150 years ago, was captured by a band of Indians and carried away into the wilderness. She lived a wild and primitive life with them for two years and then made her escape. She had been treated with respect by the Indians, but when she found out that she was to be married to the chief's son when they reached their village, one night under cover of darkness she fled into the forest. She claimed that her steps must have been guided from above as there were no trails through this country, and her sense of direction was lacking. When the Indians discovered her absence, they set foot on her trail but caught up with her too late. She had reached the Levisa Fork near a small white settlement, had screamed her lungs out and was being dragged across the river by white settlers when the pursuing Indians arrived. A short gun battle ensued, but she reached the far bank safely. Her descendants are still living there today. So much for the historical background of the Jenny Wiley State Park.

Now, as for us, we walk the hill to the boat dock and rent a small launch with outboard to try our luck in the lake. We have a nice two-hour cruise of exploration stopping in several places to fish and finally returning to the dock as the sun is setting. We have a delicious dinner in the lodge and retire to our suite to talk things over, plan the next day's trip, and so to bed.

The next day dawns bright and clear, and we are up, loaded, and off by nine o'clock. The route lies along the Levisa Fork to Paintsville, and then we turn north on a small county road to the unknown. We did finally find the creek we were looking for, donned our waders and took to the water. This was a clear limestone stream with huge trees along it and great limestone rocks and many caves. We caught large minnows and some bass, but no trout. There was a small settlement near the stream, and we figured that this portion of it had been heavily fished, so we abandoned the place and took to the car again. We made a big loop around through this countryside and noted how tidy and freshly painted were the small houses of the inhabitants. This was a far cry from pictures of Appalachia that are reproduced in the press. Paintsville and Prestonsburg also seemed to be thriving communities with no slums in evidence. The cars on the highways were new and well kept up.

We had lunch at the lodge, packed our belongings and were off on the return journey by two o'clock. We decided to stop and try our luck at Campton Lake about forty-five miles down the Mountain Parkway. This is a truly remote lake where the county has erected some nice little picnic lunch shelters and parking spaces. There is only one other fisherman present, and he shows us a string of bluegills and two rainbow trout he has already caught. We take a rough mountain path along the edge of the lake and are soon fishing. Within an hour we have in the basket ten big fat bluegills and one small rainbow, a good enough catch for the day. It is still early, and we decide to go back by way of the Red River Gorge and try our luck on Swift Creek, a wild mountain stream which flows from the high country down into the bottom of the gorge. We take to the Mountain Parkway again heading homeward, get off at Pine Ridge, and from there follow a narrow winding road down to the gorge. This country is in Daniel Boone National Forest and is full of wild game, including deer, grouse and wildcats. About six miles down this country road there is a little turn-off where we can park the car and walk down through the thick woods to Swift Creek, where the creek falls into a pool bordered by gigantic rock pillars.

Jouett and Hobbs fish with night crawlers, and I am using my lightweight fly rod with streamer flies. I don my waders and wade downstream to the pool where Jouett already has caught a nice rainbow about ten inches long. My gray ghost streamer is soon at work, and within half an hour I have three eight- to ten-inch rainbows in the creel. We decide to call it quits, reload the car and are soon driving down through the Red River Gorge. This is an unbelievably dramatic drive with the huge limestone cliffs and promontories rising hundreds of feet above the river bottom. The road finally cuts through a mountain in a narrow dark tunnel and emerges beyond into a primitive and sparsely populated countryside. It finally takes one back to the Mountain Parkway at Nada, and so on back to Lexington.

Hobbs and I sit up that evening over some good Scotch whiskey and rehash the pleasures of this outing. We decide that it is very important to have one or more hobbies. These hobbies supply a contrast to your daily routine. One such hobby should involve the outdoors, whether it be gardening, bird watching, fishing and hunting, camping, or just visiting the more remote areas of our vast country. You will meet interesting people while doing this and gain strength and courage to tackle your everyday problems. They will, I believe, become high peaks in your life as they have in mine, and sometimes they serve to set your problems in proper perspective. Why did I have that stupid argument with my wife? What are my objectives, anyway? Why am I putting off things until tomorrow which I should be doing today?

Perhaps the outdoors will not accomplish as much for every person as it has for me, but let me remind you of what David said: "I will lift up mine eyes unto the hills, from whence cometh my help."

16 | The Great Discovery

My GOLDEN YEARS started when Mary and I were married in January, 1958. I am actually writing this story on our eighteenth wedding anniversary. We have led and are still leading an exciting life with business interests, civic affairs, the outdoors, colorful social events, and children to care for.

In the 1960s, while Mary was basically occupied with the loving care of five children, the frightening spectre of old age approaching came to haunt me. When you have been very active both physically and mentally all your life, the relentless symptoms of age, which do occur, tend to depress you. All the more in my case, as I am married to a younger lady.

Then in 1970 came a truly serious crisis. A blood clot formed in an artery leading from the heart through the right side of the collarbone toward my right arm. I was rushed to the hospital, the clot broke and quick surgery saved me from having my right arm amputated. The recovery was slow and painful, as it was accompanied by spells of real mental depression. My right arm had served me so well in sports, in wartime, and in writing and painting. I felt that the only thing worse than this would have been the loss of my eyesight.

Then the will to live came to me from God, and I started to research the aging process and what could be done to delay it. One authority said you must continue to innovate, whether it be starting a new business project, a new sports interest, new social activities, or merely bird watching: any or all of these things to get you out of old routines, and so to stimulate the mind and body. Never think of retiring at any age!

Another authority said that you must sit down thoughtfully and write down two lists, i.e., your short-range objectives, and your long-range objectives. You must check them out every month to see whether you are attaining them and whether some new ones should be added.

A medical authority said that the secret to renewed youth lay in proper nutrition. Get back to basic foods: fresh vegetables, fruits, lean meats, and fresh eggs and fish. Find out from your doctor what your correct weight range should be, and put a weight scales in your bathroom. If you are going over, reduce the size of your portions at mealtimes; if under, increase them. Do not go on crash diets. Eat three meals a day and, in any event, do not cut out breakfast. Breakfast is the most important of the three, so eat a full breakfast to give you energy for the morning activities. If you do this you will not overeat at lunch.

Then I explored the various writings on the subject of physical exercise. The consensus was that, as age progresses, one should cut down on over-demanding sports and substitute such things as walking, bicycling, golf, swimming, and horseback riding, if available. Do one or more of these daily, not only on weekends. When rising from bed in the morning take ten or fifteen minutes to stretch and do some mild calisthenics to stimulate circulation. Take a short very hot shower followed by an icy cold one. I then explored books on yoga after forty. Yoga is a combination of meditation and body exercises in all sorts of positions. Select the ones you can do without straining. There were extraordinary accounts of yoga disciples who were extremely active at ages over one hundred.

Finally, I researched vitamins. I figured that the good food my wife prepared contained normal amounts of all vitamins. But one vitamin, E, had extra potential, taken in high international unit pills. Also the fluid, rubbed on minor cuts or wrinkles in the skin, would restore the skin's texture with a youthful glow. Vitamins C, B, and D also could do no harm.

With all the suggestions accumulated in the above paragraphs, all that was needed now was the will to experiment. "Okay, let's go," I said, and that day has got to be a high peak in my life, for people tell me today that I look ten years younger than I did a year ago. I realize that, to the reader, all the above will sound over-powering and a little too much to face up to. From a time point of view, I promise you that it is very practical: fifteen minutes in the morning before breakfast and forty-five minutes in the afternoon for exercise. The balance of the program has to do with nutrition and mental occupation. And don't forget to find out from a doctor what your proper weight range should be and buy a scales to check yourself out at least once weekly.

Mind you, to execute daily all of these things does require self-discipline, but you will find that this comes easier as the spectacular results become evident, when your wife starts sprucing up as she notices the attention you are getting from other ladies. She even buys you the latest in men's apparel, including swim trunks, shoes, and dressing gowns.

Upon reflecting five years later on the relative

importance of these youth-preserving measures, I am inclined to place them in the following order of importance: (1) Keep your mind innovating and not pointed toward an age of retirement. (2) Study food values and try to eliminate the poor ones from your diet. Add some vitamins. (3) Keep within five pounds of your doctor's recommended weight.

Well, my love for my wife motivated me into making myself more attractive to her, and gave me the will to learn how to live happily. What could be fairer! And these ways are within reach of the average American.

17 | The Sea around Us

THE CONCEPT of Marineland occurred to Douglas Burden and me in the mid-1930s when, as trustees of the American Museum of Natural History in New York City, we led a fierce battle against some of the old guard, in order to change the basic purposes of the museum.

These purposes had been to "collect, catalogue, and display." We wanted these changed to "collect, display, and educate." That word "educate" would lead to environmental study and man's place in the scheme of natural history, hence, what is now termed "ecology." We wanted to bring the museum to life and find a way to provide entertainment which would stimulate and educate. Both of us had already had experience in making motion pictures. Burden had produced *Feast or Famine* in the far wilderness of northwest Canada. My close friend Merian Cooper, producer of *Grass* and *Chang*, and I had formed the company, together with my cousin John Hay Whitney, which had already produced *Rebecca*, *A Star Is Born*, *Becky Sharp*, and was currently embarked on the production of *Gone with the Wind*. We believed that movies were the ideal way to display and entertain—where the audience sat in a dark room and could only see the lighted screen. Our friend, Ilia Tolstoy, came in at this time (for he had been cameraman in the making of *Feast or Fam-*

ine) and the three of us were looking for new fields to conquer. A lot about the land animals was known, but how little about life in the sea! From this idea Marineland was born.

Could we find a practical land site from which the creatures of the sea, from whales to minnows, could be captured alive? Could we transport them alive to this land base? Could we keep them alive and display them to the public? Could a shark be trained to perform tricks? Would marine scientists be sufficiently interested to attract them for serious study of the ocean depths? How much would all of this cost, and how could we get revenue to repay investors? These were the principal problems we faced.

So here, in the concept of Marineland, the pioneer instinct surfaced again. Is there a pioneering gene in our complicated chromosome structure, or is it a combination of the right one with the right egg? We in the horse-breeding industry know that there is no sure way as yet to pass along the outstanding racehorse. Otherwise, we would all be breeding Man o' Wars. You must admit that in my case, born with a silver spoon in my mouth, so to speak, it is food for thought that I have labored to pioneer in many fields all of my life. It is true that both my Whitney and Vanderbilt ancestors were pioneers. So maybe there is such a gene! Perhaps researchers can tell me?

Florida, with the Gulf Stream offshore and a good year-round climate, seemed to us the best place to start exploration. Each of us had a job to do. Ilia Tolstoy was dispatched to locate a site. I started, in the summer of 1936, catching large sharks off Montauk Point in the eastern tip of Long Island, penning them up and studying their behavior to see whether they would survive in captivity. Douglas Burden worked with the Museum of Natural History to devise a type of harpoon with syringe and drug which could tranquilize any large creature from the sea long enough to transport it to shore and then to the projected giant oceanariums we visualized. By late summer Tolstoy returned with the great news that he had found a practical site for the type of operation we envisioned. The site lay fourteen miles south of St. Augustine, Florida, at a spot where the inland waterways came within several hundred yards of the Atlantic Ocean. Matanzas Inlet was only two miles north of the location, so fish caught in the sea or inland waterways could be transported by boat with minimum delay to the site. This much was ideal.

The problems, however, were: a one-lane sand road from St. Augustine south, no great centers of population nearby, the site was presently flooded with brackish sea water, no telephone service, and no supply of fresh or drinkable water. What we would need immediately, before even deciding to purchase the land, was a top-grade engineer to advise us whether these and other technical problems were surmountable.

I do not recall exactly how Newton Ebaugh was discovered by our group, but that dedicated engineer, who is still with us in the year 1975, was hired and shortly thereafter gave us the signal to go ahead.

It then took us nearly two years to build the first oceanarium in the world and to put an organization together to operate it. We originally called it Marine Studios, but today it is known as Marineland. Our office was at "Ducky" Glicks' bar in St. Augustine, and our key personnel were housed in a wood-framed building within the Mellon compound on Matanzas Inlet by the sea.

During the construction period, two events of great importance to our future occurred. Number one was the unexpected interest shown by marine biologists and scientists in what we were doing. This interest was so keen that we enlarged the plans for the laboratory, and found ourselves booked for a year after opening with visiting scientists.

Number two was even more unexpected. One day a man walked out of the bush, so to speak, and said that he knew by instinct that he could train dolphins, more commonly called porpoises, to perform beautiful and exciting tricks. He said that he knew that the dolphin was the friend of man and would be a far greater drawing card than the shark. I will admit that we had not gotten very far with our sharks, other than to keep them alive, so the man's utter confidence struck a responsive note and we hired him.

We immediately set about catching dolphins, and Fred Lyons and Mitch Leipsig set about training them. By the time that we were ready to open the exhibit to the public, the dolphins were jumping out of the water to catch fish from Mitch's hands in a spectacular fashion, and we had a huge rectangular oceanarium filled with every kind of semi-tropical fish from huge sharks and rays to tiny reef fish.

We finally opened Marine Studios in 1938, and to our great surprise some twenty thousand people surged through the gates. Traffic was bumper-to-bumper over the road from St. Augustine, which had been paved and a decent bridge built across the inlet. One of our directors, Ralph Poole, who had charge of public rela-

tions, seized this opportunity to give us national publicity, and from that day forth we found ourselves in
a growing and thriving business.

Then came World War II, and Marineland was
taken over by the U.S. Coast Guard and closed to the
public. They did make a contribution to the war effort
by developing a shark repellent which aviators could
attach to their uniforms; if shot down and dumped in
the sea, the repellent kept sharks away. All the fish in
the huge tanks were released, and so when the war
finally ended in 1945 we had to go about restocking the
entire exhibits.

In the postwar period we started new programs to
enlarge our scope and improve the exhibits and shows.
The marine lab work suffered a decline, although we
did keep a permanent staff doing more or less routine
work on the specimens on hand.

Then came the tourist and housing booms in Florida in the late sixties and early seventies. Also came
Disney World and other huge tourist attractions. We
had to meet this competition, so our directors decided
to launch a six-million-dollar expansion program. All of
our directors wanted the company to get back into
serious scientific research of the oceans. The world
population was growing so fast that it was problemati-
cal whether people could be fed from the land. Fish
populations were diminishing and the seas were being
polluted. The art of fertilizing fish eggs and, so to speak,
developing fish-raising gardens of the sea was just being
dreamed of. And lastly, no creature from the seas de-
velops that dread disease cancer—might we discover
the reason why!

On several occasions I had met the president of

the University of Florida, Stephen O'Connell. I had
been very impressed with his ability, and with his fore-
sight and goals for the university, so I telephoned him,
told him I was coming to Gainesville to stay with Newton Ebaugh, and could I have an appointment with
him? He said, "Come and spend the night with me and
I'll show you around."

Well, I accepted and went, and that evening after
a nice home-cooked dinner, we launched the Whitney
Marine Research Laboratory of the University of Florida. The university foundation would finance one-half
of the cost of construction and myself one-half.

When I reported the good news to my directors,
there was great enthusiasm and renewed vigor in future
planning.

Nineteen seventy-three was a boom year at Marineland. The sky was our limit. Disney World actually
brought us many visitors. The university had desig-
nated Dr. Samuel Gurin as director of the lab, and
through his great zeal the building was finished and
partially equipped by the end of the year.

Then came 1974 with the gas shortage panic, and
confusion became general. But in January we had
planned the formal dedication of the new laboratory,
and we went through with it. Lawmakers, dignitaries
from all over the state, and Nobel prize winners in
marine research were present. The interim president of
the University of Florida, Mr. E. T. York, Jr., presided.

He gave the welcoming speech on behalf of the
university: "We are deeply indebted to Mr. Whitney
for his most generous personal gift of $150,000 to the
University of Florida Foundation, Inc., and to the officers and directors of the foundation for generating the

remaining $150,000 necessary for the construction of this facility. They have placed a great challenge before us, and we pledge that we will use this facility for the furtherance of all mankind."

I spoke next with these opening lines, "Today, January 30, 1974, I am seeing the culmination of dreams which started in 1936." In closing my address, I congratulated the University of Florida and my own board of directors for the faith in the future they had demonstrated in establishing this laboratory of marine research at Marineland, Florida.

Dr. Sam Gurin, host for the dedication, summarized his feelings by concluding, "We have built what I hope will become an institute for advanced study in marine biomedical research."

William Palmer, Jr., president of Florida Foundation, Inc., accepted the Whitney lab on behalf of the foundation and said, "The gifts from Mr. Whitney and Marineland, Inc., will make possible a research facility and research programs that would not have been possible otherwise."

And then, to conclude the ceremonies, our longtime friend Father Mike Gannon gave the dedicatory prayer. This milestone was the high peak in my forty years of active direction of the founding and growth of Marineland. We have always had a family-type entertaining and educational exhibit. Now, as many believe, we are in a position to contribute to the world knowledge of the sea around us, which may be crucial to our survival.

18 | Royal Visit, 1974

LOVING THE bluegrass country so much, I thought the one hundredth running of the Kentucky Derby in the spring of 1974 deserved something extra special, but I didn't dream it might be a royal visit. The authorities chose Mary and me to entertain the Princess Margaret of England and her husband Lord Snowdon in our home. We had met the royal couple before, and, being the gifted hostess she is, Mary swung into action almost as soon as we had word that the royal couple would stay with us for four days.

Actually, I had met the princess twice before. The first time was when I went to London in post–World War II days as a representative of the American Jockey Club. Our American ambassador, Winthrop Aldrich, gave a magnificent dinner dance in her honor, and I had the distinct honor of leading off the ball by dancing a waltz with the princess. The waltz has never been my forte, but we enjoyed it nonetheless. The second time I met Her Royal Highness was in 1964. Mary and I were spending a happy day on a tiny beach on the island of Spetzapula in the Aegean Sea, where we were swimming and picnicking with our hosts, the Stavros Niarchos. Princess Margaret had only recently married Anthony Armstrong-Jones and they, too, were guests of the Niarchos. My sister Barbara and her husband, George Headley, were with us aboard the yacht *Niki*, exploring the Greek islands, and none of us has forgotten that delightful day.

It would take much too long to go into all the details of the preparations for the royal visit, or to give the proper credit to all the people involved in the planning and entertaining. The security problems alone would fill a small volume. Nineteen seventy-four was a turbulent year in the world's history, and the last thing desired by the United States government was to have the royal couple injured or killed during their goodwill visit to our country. To facilitate security, even Mary and I wore identification badges there on the grounds of our own farm.

The royal couple arrived on a Thursday, and every bit of their stay was minutely planned until their departure on Sunday afternoon. Social parties, press interviews, visits to horse farms followed one another from morning into nighttime. Princess Margaret and her husband, who preferred to be called Tony, were housed in our guest house which, more than one hundred years ago—long before my family had acquired the property —had been a slave house. Mary has transformed it into a perfectly charming little house and the princess's suite on the second floor—all ivory white and delicate blue—seemed to please our royal visitor very much. The press appeared to be titillated by the thought of a royal princess reared in Buckingham Palace now residing in a former slave house, and each time the subject arose, as it did many times in the course of interviews, Her Royal Highness would smile most fetchingly and say, "Well, it certainly doesn't look like a slave house now."

Although Princess Margaret's chief interest was in the horses and the horse farms of the bluegrass country, she was nevertheless enchanted with the doll house Mary had built for our daughter, Cornelia. It is an exact replica of our main house on the horse farm, and since Windsor Castle contains one of the world's most famous doll houses, Her Royal Highness expressed an interest in seeing our less historic but no less beloved doll house. I recall that she was especially intrigued with the miniature books in the doll house library, each one a readable replica of a book to be found in the library in the main house. And the princess laughed delightedly at the sight of the homemade sterling silver mint julep cups, no larger than an infant's fingernail, filled with ice and mint and set on a silver tray on one of the tiny terrace tables, for that day Her Royal Highness had tasted her very first mint julep.

Tony, of course, had his own special interests and occupations. A professional photographer, inventor of mechanical devices, and a producer of motion pictures, he was full of amusing stories and repartee. It would have been so easy, I thought, for him to have led the secluded life his position called for. But he had chosen to maintain his identity and pursue his business interests. That the English press criticized him for this had apparently only made him work that much harder.

The big event was to be the Kentucky Derby, but for me—since I had no horse in the Derby—it was the race before the Derby that mattered most, the Debutante Stakes for two-year-old fillies, for which I had prepped my most promising filly, Sun and Snow.

Derby Day, Saturday, May 4, dawned bright and clear. Until then the princess had not been on public display, and a crowd of some 150,000 was expected at Churchill Downs in Louisville. We were all rather on edge that morning since a threat on her life had recently been received. Had every step to protect her been taken?

Promptly at eight-thirty the cavalcade of cars with their police and secret service escorts were lined up at our front door for the eighty-mile drive to Louisville. I was to ride in car number one with the princess and her lady-in-waiting, Lady Wills; my wife Mary and Tony, Lord Snowdon, in car number two; and then the many other dignitaries and staff in order of protocol.

By Derby Day we had become used to traveling this way together and so, although the princess always maintained her dignity, the conversation was relaxed and easy. Spring had been a little late that year and so the bluegrass countryside was not yet in full bloom. Still it is always a spectacular drive with its farms and wild stretches of primitive country. Such a peaceful landscape, and so typical of the best of rural America.

Princess Margaret chatted enthusiastically about the dinner dance Mary and I had given in her honor the night before. We had erected a bridge over our indoor swimming pool where we had the receiving line, and on the water floated beautiful swans fashioned of feathers. The princess had specifically requested that we conduct the dance in American style, which meant that the men present could cut in on her while she was dancing. And cut in they most certainly did! She never could get more than a few steps with any one man. This was a new experience for her. She found it utterly delightful. The men even came to her table while she was dining and asked her to dance. "I certainly had a ball last night," she told me while our car sped through the countryside, "and I do like your American custom, but there were some fellows I should have liked to have danced with longer."

"There were a lot of men who said the same thing about you," I replied. Lady Wills, a charming, vivacious woman herself, added, "I have never seen the princess so thoroughly at home. Your Kentucky friends are so warm and hospitable."

"May I add," the princess continued, "I have never seen a more beautifully decorated or organized party. Your wife Mary never ceases to amaze me. She has warmth and taste and a real knack of making people feel wanted and at ease. When Tony and I got back to your guest house we sat up and talked for nearly half an hour. You will be surprised, Mr. Whitney, when I tell you what I said to him."

"Did you tell him what a hit he, too, was at the party?"

"Certainly not, he's spoiled enough," she quipped. "I told him that, if I were not who I am, I would like to buy a small farm in Kentucky and live with these hospitable people forever and, believe it or not, he agreed—for once."

"Well, Ma'am, we did," I exclaimed. "I brought Mary here for a weekend and we've returned for fifteen years and never regretted it."

After luncheon at the home of Mr. and Mrs. Barry Bingham in Louisville, which gave our royal guests the opportunity of meeting many more people from Louisville and other parts of Kentucky, the cavalcade of cars got under way again and, as we approached the Downs, the feeling of excitement grew. The princess, aware of my interest in the Debutante Stakes, asked me if I thought Sun and Snow had a chance to win. I replied that I thought she had a chance.

We alighted from our cars and began the walk to the grandstands, the path lined with national guardsmen assigned to make way for our party. The crowds pressed up against the walkway and I could hear the comments: "Why, she's much more beautiful than her pictures!" "What a doll that Tony is!" "Welcome to Kentucky!" "Come back and see us!" Happily, I did not hear one vicious or nasty word said.

A special box had been prepared for about thirty of us who were the royal couple's official hosts and entourage. I sat on the princess's right, the British ambassador on her left, then Mary and Lord Snowdon.

I have never seen such a huge crowd as there was that day. Even the infield was jammed. A bugle sounded and the horses started coming out on the track for the running of the Debutante Stakes. We'd made it just in the nick of time.

Sun and Snow won in a blazing finish to wild applause. And when I stood up to take a bow, Princess Margaret arose, too, and kissed me on the cheek as the press cameras clicked. Mary had to rush down to the finish line with a police escort and receive the beautiful trophy, while the crowd roared its approval. That was the high point of the day for me, though the Derby was exciting as always.

When our royal guests and their entourage departed the following afternoon, our household staff lined up with tears in their eyes to say goodbye, and the princess gave each one of them a beautiful gift. Dear Carrie, our cook, capsuled the feelings of us all most succinctly, I think, when a little later that day she turned to Mary and said, "Mrs. Whitney, they were the nicest guests you all ever had here."

19 | Rock Fever

EVERY YEAR every man wonders how to spend his vacation. It is true that Mary and I have four homes in the United States, but each of them has business connections, with an office nearby and telephones ringing. So some ten years ago we started looking for a hideaway where our little family could spend a few weeks together in peace and quiet.

About five years later we found the ideal place on the island of Mallorca in the Mediterranean Sea, nearly halfway between Spain and Africa. So we bought two and a half acres of land on a hillside with a small renovated farmhouse, a tiny guest house for our children, a swimming pool, and an adequate garage. From the terrace one could see the beautiful bay at Puerto Pollenca, the white houses of the little village, and the jagged mountain peaks beyond.

Much needed to be done to furnish the house and improve the grounds, and each year we have enjoyed doing it, Mary the house, and I the grounds. The themes we followed were comfort and seclusion, and at last we have achieved it.

Time, as we think of it in the United States, does not apply to island life. Some call it *rock fever*. On Mallorca the climate is semi-tropical. Nothing momentous or exciting ever happens. We have a few friends in our neighborhood, and we dine together occasionally. We swim in the gorgeous sea on remote and isolated beaches. We drive our Seat station wagon to shop around, try out country restaurants, or find good picnic sites. For the most part, we lead very much a family life, and the cooking is done by Mary, with Heather and Cornelia assisting. Mallorcan peasants take care of the house and grounds, and señor Ramon Castro, as agent, directs the affairs of the tiny estate.

On June 20, 1974, Mary, Heather, Cornelia and I fly to this remote island for a three-week vacation.

We are greeted at our house with much kissing and embracing. The house and grounds are in superlative condition. There is not a cloud in the azure sky, and the temperature is about eighty degrees. Señor Castro advises me that he received my letter and has reserved a table for us at La Longa for dinner at nine o'clock. By the time we have unpacked, had a swim and set things to our liking, the shadows of evening are ascending the mountains, and it is time to drive to Puerto Pollenca. We have changed into informal summer clothes, and our Seat station wagon is ready. It is only a ten-minute drive, and I park the car on the fishing wharf right next to La Longa restaurant. The little yacht basin is full of boats of all kinds, nothing, mind you, over thirty or forty feet in length. We are greeted by the proprietor, Mr. Salvatore, and shown to our table.

The place is decorated in simple elegance: the eight tables with their red tablecloths, the native glassware and china, and the dim lighting effects. An aquarium full of lobsters and fish gives proof that we are actually on the sea. In the old days this was a fish market, and people came to the wharf to bid for the fish as they were unloaded from the boats.

Tonight there are only two other tables occupied

as yet, for of course we are a little early according to Spanish customs. But we order drinks, smoke a cigarette and peruse the beautiful menu. We talk of our busy life for the past two months and of our much-needed rest to come. Then I walk out on the pier, and Mr. Salvatore follows me out. I ask him how business is, and he says that for him it is the same as he only caters to a regular clientele, not to tourists. The hotels are having a bad time, but perhaps it will be better late in the summer.

The wind has now completely dropped, it is dark, and the lights of the village are reflected in the aquamarine water. As soon as summer weather arrives, he tells me, he is putting some tables out on the pier behind the bar, and we will be able to dine under the stars.

I then rejoin the family, and we order dinner. I have a cream of tomato soup, then a fresh fish from the sea followed by chocolate and vanilla ice cream. A delicious bottle of white Monopole wine relaxes us, and we talk of many things, including cabbages and kings. We tell the girls about Princess Margaret's visit with us over the Kentucky Derby in May. The girls tell us about their school life in Switzerland, their friends of many nationalities, and the sports and parties in which they participate. Then we all review our recent stay in Trujillo, Spain, and in particular the day, only five days ago, when señora de Franco, the first lady of Spain, came to our house for lunch.

I tell Heather and Cornelia what impressed Mrs. Franco the most. It was not the great job of reconstruction and furnishing of that ancient palace, although she was highly complimentary about this. It was that contrary to everything she had read and heard about family life in the United States, it was very obvious to her that the Whitney family's life was totally different. She said to her friend, Carmen de Salles, "The Whitneys are like a Spanish family. They are very close to their children. They love their children. They have taught them good manners, and the children are happy. Why does the press tell us that family life does not really exist anymore in the United States?" Carmen did not really have an answer.

"Is this really true?" I then ask Heather and Cornelia. "I am afraid, Daddy," they say, "that on this subject the American press is pretty accurate. There are exceptions, yes, but most kids don't have a real family life the way we do."

"How come?" say I.

"Well, you see it's this way. You work in the daytime, Daddy, but Mummy stays at home. Yes, she goes out to lunch occasionally with her girl friends or goes shopping, but most of these kids' mothers are at the country club all day playing golf or tennis or bridge. Some of them are on ladies' committees of some kind or other, and then they go out an awful lot to dinner and movies. There is no real home life for the kids."

Then Mary cuts in and says, "My first duty is to be a good housewife. I do serve on worthwhile civic committees if they don't take too much of my time. We hardly ever go out more than twice a week at night, so that we can be with you. What is a family for if you don't want to enjoy being together?"

"I feel that way too," chime in the girls, and then I add, "Why do you suppose I come home nearly every day for lunch? It is because Mummy sees that I get a delicious meal. She either cooks it herself or teaches

Carrie how. And on vacation we always take you with us to New York, Saratoga, the Adirondacks or Marineland. It's our way of life; we enjoy it that way. I guess that's why we do it. We love our own friends, too, and, come to think of it, our very best friends lead the same kind of life as we do. What is it they say? Oh, yes, 'Birds of a feather flock together.' Let's have a drink to it." So we all raise our glasses and say, "Salud."

And so the time goes by until I glance at my watch and see that it is nearly midnight. I pay the modest check, and we wander out on the pier. All is quiet outside, for the little village has gone to sleep. I feel relaxed and in harmony with our friendly and peaceful surroundings.

In Mallorca our family derives happiness from the more primitive and basic way of life. My God, I am beginning to get rock fever on the first evening here. Well, remember that great hero of the Trojan war, Ulysses. He left his home ten years before Troy actually was conquered. Then he set sail for home and took another ten years to reach it. His home on the island of Ithaca was actually only about a ten days' voyage. It seems that on every island he stopped, he got rock fever in one form or another and had difficulty tearing himself away.

I thought to myself, "Hey, Whitney, if you're thinking like this the first night on this island, better watch out when your vacation ends three weeks from now."

I know that this homespun evening will not sound to many like a high peak, but it is to me, and I would be remiss if I did not include it.

Epilogue

THE READER must have noticed that these stories omit the names of many people who have been part of the episodes. It was impossible to name them all in my short story format, so in almost all cases I decided to omit names. I hope my many friends and acquaintances will understand.

I also hope they will give a better picture of the American scene and the ways of the wealthy than is usually depicted in the news media, television and the movies. I am very proud to be an American. I am gratified to have taken an active part in the varied activities of my country: business growth, sports, the arts, politics and war. I have tried "to meet with triumph and disaster, and treat those two imposters just the same."

If I could pass along any bits of advice to aid others, I believe that the first would be that "idle hands are the Devil's playground." When your retirement age arrives, do not think of yourself sitting happily in a rocking chair on your front porch. I have seen too many men who did this wither away and die prematurely. On the contrary, think of the freedom you will have to innovate new ventures or hobbies. You will be the happier for it and so will your family. Productive years can start at sixty-five instead of ending there. Equally important for your peace of mind would be to continually thank God for your blessings. My blessings have been that, since I married Mary in 1958, I have learned to love married life, to continue my business and other interests, and to encourage her many many talents. And finally, we feel that the love and discipline we have given the children have rewarded us: M'Lou is happily married, Hobbs and Hank have good jobs in industry, and Heather and Cornelia will be graduating from college and high school in Switzerland. We are indeed fortunate to have these and many other blessings, one of which is that we are Americans.

HIGH PEAKS has been set in Linotype Caledonia
with Palatino Semibold for display.

Composition and printing by Heritage Printers, Inc.
Binding by The Delmar Company

Design by Ellsworth Taylor